Pocket Guide to EDINBURGH

Published by the Automobile Association,
Fanum House, Basingstoke, Hampshire RG21 2EA

Editor: Betty Sheldrick
Copy Editors: Karin Fancett, Barry Francis
Editorial Contributors: Jim Bowman (Edinburgh's Villages); The Cadies (City Walks) Iain Crawford (The Story of Edinburgh, The Festival and the Arts, Famous Residents); Albert Morris (The Royal Mile); Basil Skinner (Capital Buildings); Gilbert Summers (City Centre: Places to Visit)

Directory compiled by Pam Stagg

The publishers would like to thank the Scottish Tourist Board and Edinburgh District Council for their help in the preparation of this book.

Maps produced by the Cartographic Department of the Automobile Association

---

Filmset by Vantage Photosetting Co Ltd, Eastleigh and London, England

Printed and bound in Great Britain UK by: Purnell Book Production Limited, member of the BPCC Group

The contents of this publication are believed correct at the time of printing. Nevertheless, the Publishers cannot accept responsibility for errors or omissions, or for changes in details given beforehand.

© The Automobile Association 1988

All rights reserved. No part of this publication may be reproduced, stored in a retrieval system or transmitted in any form or by any means – electronic, mechanical, photocopying, recording or otherwise – unless the written permission of the Publisher has been given beforehand

---

ISBN 0 86145 673 4
AA Reference 53471

Produced and distributed in the United Kingdom by the Publishing Division of the Automobile Association, Fanum House, Basingstoke, Hampshire, RG21 2EA

Contents

4	**Introduction**
5	**About this Book**
6	**Edinburgh City Plan**
8	**Street Index**
11	**Features**
	The Story of Edinburgh 12
	Capital Buildings 19
	The Royal Mile 23
	Edinburgh's Villages 29
	The Festival & the Arts 34
	Famous Residents 38
45–62	**Places to Visit**
63	**City Walks**
	The Bridges and Calton Hill 64
	Greyfriars Kirkyard 66
	Cramond Village 68
	The Water of Leith 70
	Princes Street 72
	The New Town 74
77	**Directory**
	Using the Directory 78
	How to get there 79
	Accommodation 79
	Eating & Drinking Out 81
	Places to Visit 81
	Entertainment 85
	Recreation & Sport 86
	Shopping 88
	Transport 89
	Useful information 90
93	**Index**

Introduction

Whichever way you enter Edinburgh it is immediately impressive, the Castle on its high rock floating above the roofs and steeples, the turrets and towers of the Old Town jagged along the spur which falls from its battlements to the Palace of Holyroodhouse.

Later you will discover the New Town, which has been described as 'the most extensive example of a romantic classical city in the world', and its air of prosperous serenity.

It is almost impossible to select just a few of the highlights of a visit to Edinburgh, but this compact little book contains everything a visitor will want to know. Designed for easy reference, the guide is divided into four sections, each packed with detailed information which will help readers discover the charm and beauty of this ancient capital.

Within these pages there is also a considerable amount of practical information, plus a street map of the centre of Edinburgh showing places of interest, making this handy book an ideal guide to the city.

About this Book

Edinburgh Pocket Guide, designed to be the complete guide for tourist or resident, contains the following sections.

City Plan — A large-scale map of the city centre, with a street index and places of interest clearly shown.

Features — Written by local experts, these introductory articles cover subjects of special importance in the city — from its fascinating history and striking buildings to its famous residents and world-renowned Festival.

Places to Visit — Here places of interest, listed alphabetically, are described in detail. Each entry includes its street name, so it can easily be located on the street plan on page 6. For opening times and practical information refer to the Directory.

City Walks — Six walks, with step-by-step route directions, have been carefully planned to take in the best of the city.

Directory — Fifteen pages packed with useful information grouped into sections (see page 77). All you need to know about where to eat and stay, recreation, shops, sports and services, plus the addresses and opening times for all the places of interest described in the book.

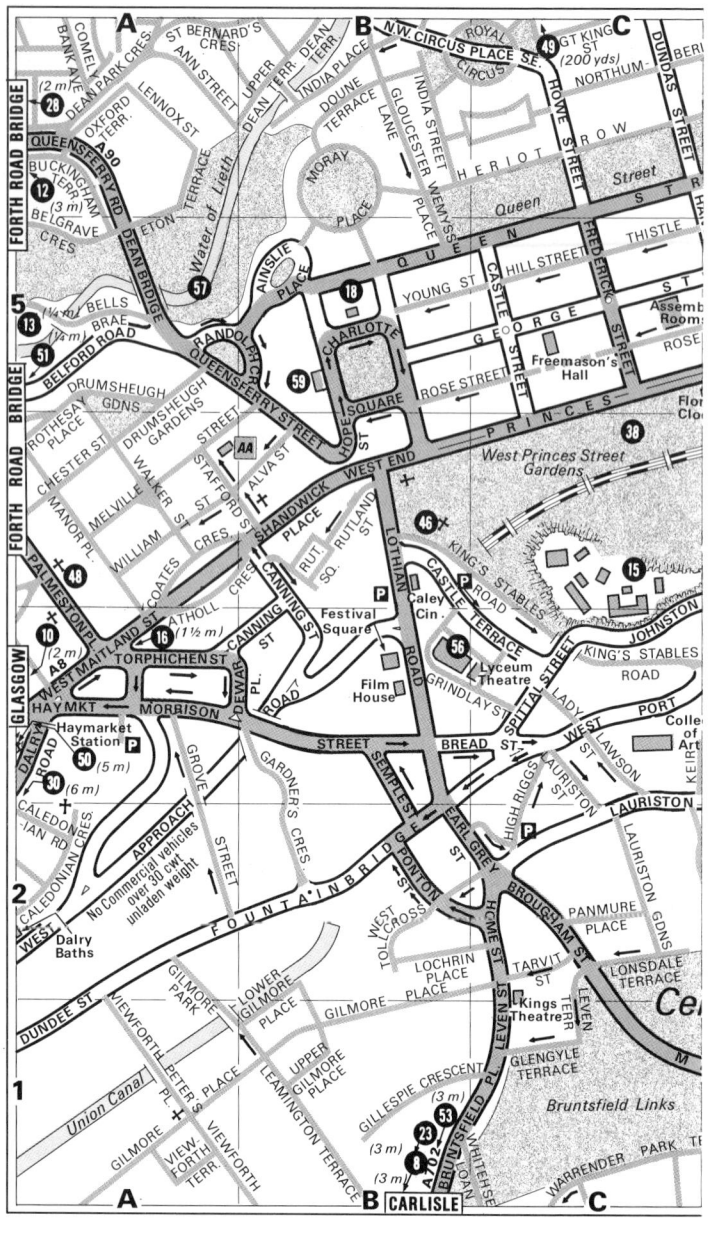

Key to Places of Interest

1 Calton Hill	F6
2 Camera Obscura and Outlook Tower	D4
3 Canongate Church	F5
4 Canongate Tolbooth	F5
5 Childhood, Museum of	E4
6 City Art Centre	E4
7 City Chambers	E4
8 Colinton	B1
9 Commonwealth Pool, Royal	F1
10 Corstorphine	A3

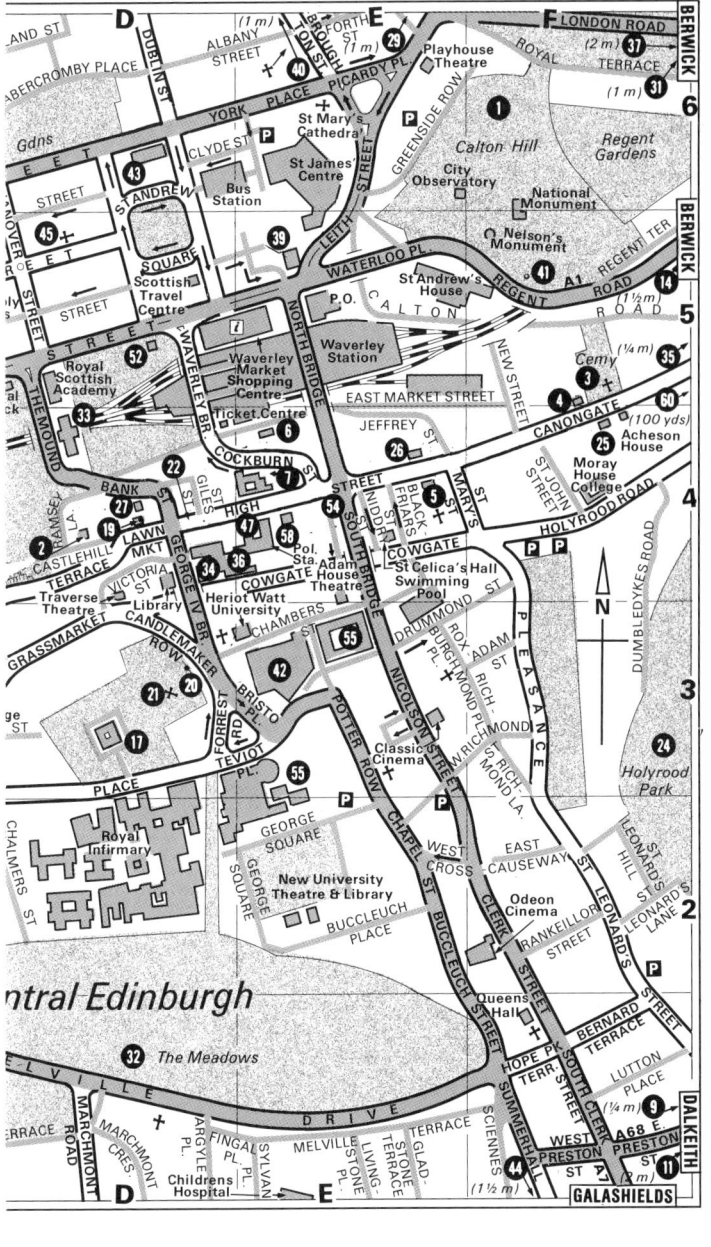

11 Craigmillar Castle	F1	18 Georgian School, The	B5
12 Cramond	A6	19 Gladstone's Land	D4
13 Dean Village	A5	20 Greyfriars Bobby	D3
14 Duddingston	F5	21 Greyfriars Church	D3
15 Edinburgh Castle	C4	22 Heart of Midlothian	D4
16 Edinburgh Zoo	A3	23 Hillend Ski Centre	B1
17 George Heriot's School	D3	24 Holyrood Park & Arthur's Seat	F3

25 Huntly House	F4
26 John Knox House	E4
27 Lady Stair's House	D4
28 Lauriston Castle	A6
29 Leith	E6
30 Malleny Gardens	A3
31 Meadowbank Sports Centre	F6
32 The Meadows	D1
33 National Gallery of Scotland	D4
34 National Library of Scotland	D4
35 Palace of Holyrood House	F5
36 Parliament House	D4-E4
37 Portobello	F6
38 Princes Street & The Gardens	C4
39 Register House	E5
40 Royal Botanic Gardens	E6
41 Royal High School	F5
42 Royal Museum of Scotland (Chambers Street)	E3
43 Royal Museum of Scotland (Queen Street)	D6
44 Royal Observatory	F1
45 St Andrew's Church	D5
46 St Cuthbert's Church	B4
47 St Giles Church	E4
48 St Mary's Cathedral	A4
49 St Stephen's Church	C6
50 Scottish Agricultural Museum	A3
51 Scottish National Gallery of Modern Art	A5
52 Scott Monument	D5
53 Swanston	B1
54 Tron Church	E4
55 University of Edinburgh	E3
56 Usher Hall	B3
57 Water of Leith	A5
58 Wax Museum	E4
59 West Register House	B5
60 White Horse Close	F5

Key to Town Plan

AA Recommended roads	▬
Other roads	—
Restricted roads	-- --
Buildings of interest	Station ▣
Churches	†
Car parks	P
Parks and open spaces	▨
AA Service Centre	AA

Street Index and Grid Reference Central Edinburgh

Abercromby Place	C6-D6
Adam Street	F3
Ainslie Place	B5
Albany Street	D6-E6
Alva Street	A4-B4
Ann Street	A6
Argyle Place	D1
Athol Crescent	A3-A4-B4
Bank Street	D4
Belford Road	A5
Belgrave Crescent	A5
Bells Brae	A5
Bernard Terrace	F1
Blackfriars Street	E4
Bread Street	B3-C3
Bristo Place	D3-E3
Brougham Street	C2
Broughton Street	E6
Bruntsfield Place	B1-C1
Buccleuch Place	E2
Buccleauch Street	E2-F2-F1
Buckingham Terrace	A5-A6
Caledonian Crescent	A2
Caledonian Road	A2
Calton Road	E5-F5
Candlemaker Row	D3
Canning Street	A3-B3-B4
Canongate	E4-F4-F5
Castle Hill	D4
Castle Street	C5
Castle Terrace	B4-B3-C3
Chalmers Street	C2-D2
Chambers Street	D3-E3
Charlotte Square	B4-B5
Chapel Street	E2
Chester Street	A4
Clerk Street	F1-F2
Clyde Street	D6-E6
Coates Crescent	A4-B4
Cockburn Street	D4-E4
Comely Bank Avenue	A6
Cowgate	D4-E4-F4
Dalry Road	A3
Dean Bridge	A5
Dean Park Crescent	A6
Dean Terrace	B6
Dewar Place	A3-B3
Doune Terrace	B6
Drummond Street	E3-F3-F4
Drumsheugh Gardens	A4-A5
Dublin Street	D6
Dumbiedykes Road	F3-F4
Dundas Street	C6
Dundee Street	A1-A2
Earl Grey Street	B2-C2
East Cross Causeway	F2
East Market Street	E5-E4-F4-F5
East Preston Street	F1
Eton Terrace	A5-A6
Fingal Place	D1-E1
Forrest Road	D3
Fountain Bridge	A2-B2-B3-C3

Street	Grid
Frederick Street	C5
Forth Street	E6
Gardener's Crescent	B2-B3
George IV Bridge	D3-D4
George Square	E2
George Street	B5-C5-D5
Gillespie Crescent	B1-C1
Gilmore Park	A1-A2
Gilmore Place	A1-B1-B2-C2
Gladstone Terrace	E1
Glengyle Terrace	C1
Gloucester Lane	B6
Grass Market	D3
Great King Street	C6
Greenside Row	E6-F6
Grindley Street	B3-C3
Grove Street	A2-A3
Hanover Street	C6-D6-D5
Hay Market	A3
Heriot Row	B6-C6
High Riggs	C2-C3
High Street	D4-E4
Hill Street	C5
Holyrood Road	F4
Home Street	C2
Hope Park Terrace	F1
Hope Street	B4
Howe Street	C6
India Place	B6
India Street	B6
Jeffrey Street	E4
Johnston Terrace	C3-C4-D4
Kier Street	C3-D3
King's Stables Road	B4-C4-C3
Lady Lawson Street	C3
Lauriston Gardens	C2
Lauriston Place	C2-C3-D3
Lauriston Street	C2-C3
Lawn Market	D4
Leamington Terrace	A1-B1
Leith Street	E5-E6
Lennox Street	A6
Leven Street	C1-C2
Leven Terrace	C1-C2
Livingtone Place	E1
Lochrin Place	B2-C2
London Road	F6
Lonsdale Terrace	C2
Lothian Road	B3-B4
Lower Gilmore Place	B1-B2
Lutton Place	F1
Manor Place	A4
Marchmont Crescent	D1
Marchmont Road	D1
Market Street	D4-E4
Melville Drive	C2-C1-D1-E1-F1
Melville Street	A4-B4-B5
Melville Terrace	E1-F1
Moray Place	B5-B6
Morriston Street	A3-B3
New Street	F4-F5
Nicolson Street	E3-E2-F2
Niddry Street	E4
North Bridge	E4-E5
North West Circus Place	B6
Northumberland Street	C6-D6
Oxford Terrace	A6
Palmerston Place	A3-A4
Panmure Place	C2
Picardy Place	E6
Pleasance	F3-F4
Ponton Street	B2-C2
Potter Row	E2-E3
Princes Street	B4-C4-C5-D5-E5
Queen Street	B5-C5-C6-D6
Queensferry Road	A5-A6
Queensferry Street	A5-B5-B4
Ramsey Lane	D4
Randolph Crescent	A5-B5
Rankeillor Street	F2
Regent Road	E5-F5
Regent Terrace	F5
Richmond Lane	F2-F3
Richmond Place	E3-F3
Rose Street	B5-C5-D5
Rothesay Place	A4-A5
Roxbury Place	E3
Royal Circus	B6-C6
Royal Terrace	E6-F6
Rutland Square	B4
Rutland Street	B4
St Andrew Square	D5-D6
St Bernard's Crescent	A6-B6
St Giles Street	D4
St John Street	F4
St Leonards Hill	F2
St Leonards Lane	F2
St Leonard's Street	F1-F2
St Mary's Street	E4-F4
St Peter Place	A1
Sciennes	F1
Semples Street	B2-B3
Shandwick Place	B4
South Bridge	E3-E4
South Clerk Street	F1
South East Circus Place	C6
Spittal Street	C3
Stafford Street	A4-B4
Summerhall	F1
Sylvan Place	E1
Tarvit Street	C2
Teviot Place	D3-E3
Thistle Street	C5-D5-D6
Torphichen Street	A3
The Mound	D4-D5
Upper Dean Terrace	B6
Upper Gilmore Place	B1
Victoria Street	D4
Viewforth	A1-B1
Viewforth Terrace	A1
Walker Street	A4-A5
Warrender Park Terrace	C1-D1
Waterloo Place	E5
Waverley Bridge	D4-D5
Wemyss Place	B5-B6
West Approach Road	A2-A3-B3
West Cross-Causeway	E2
West End	B4
West Maitland Street	A3-A4
West Port	C3
West Preston Street	F1
West Richmond Street	E3-F3
West Tollcross	B2
Whitehouse Loan	B1-C1
William Street	A4
York Place	D6-E6
Young Street	B5-C5

FEATURES

Pocket Guide to EDINBURGH

FEATURES • FEATURES

The Story of Edinburgh

The story of Edinburgh begins with the Rock. It was formed between the mountains and the sea from the old volcanic caldera of the Lothian valley with its lava slides and basalt plugs choking the throats of the ancient volcanoes, shaped later into crags and valleys by the floes of the Ice Age.

CHANGING PLACES

Edinburgh was not the 'capital' of Scotland, in the modern sense, until the end of the Middle Ages. Before then the capital was wherever the king and his court happened to be at the time. Edinburgh was only one of those centres but the Castle appears to have been a favourite residence of Scottish kings from about the 11th century.

This rock on which the Castle now towers over the heart of Edinburgh, commands the sea-gate to Scotland in the east and the march route north, trod by the Romans, Saxons and the English.

From the earliest days on this rock, Dun Edin (named perhaps for Edwin, a victorious Northumbrian king in the 7th century, or maybe the Gaelic title for the 'fortress of the hill-slope'), inevitably there crouched a castle—a fortress guarding the most vulnerable approaches to Scotland.

For 1,300 years it has been a refuge and a defiance to invaders. In the 5th century the Picts called it by a gentler title, Mynyd Eidden—Maidens' or Virgins' Castle—because they kept their daughters there, away from the rabble.

Edinburgh owes its existence to the supposed invincibility of this fortress and today its oldest building stands on its rock 300ft above the main thoroughfare, Princes Street.

Although there is evidence of Iron Age settlements on and around Arthur's Seat, Edinburgh's domestic mountain at the foot of the Royal Mile, St Margaret's Chapel is the oldest still extant structure and its origins coincide happily with the emergence of Edinburgh as Scotland's capital. It was built by David I, sixth son of the saintly Queen Margaret, the Hungarian-born English princess who married Macbeth's conqueror, Malcolm Canmore, when he moved the Scottish capital from Dunfermline to Edinburgh in 1124.

Queen Margaret exercised a civilising influence on the Scottish court and its king and was largely responsible for the assimilation of the old Celtic Church into the Church of Rome. She was canonised by Pope Innocent IV in 1251 and this casket of stone, on the highest place on the Castle Rock, is her memorial.

In the 30 years before David came to the throne there had been six kings, but he replaced the turbulence and strife of those times with order and peace.

Educated in England and more Norman than Scots, David, a pious and orderly man, introduced the feudal system to Scotland, built a number of abbeys and founded the city of Edinburgh round the Castle Rock. At first his new capital was little more than a village but when he built the Abbey of the Holy Rood at the end of the basalt spur which runs like a wedge from the Castle to the foot of Arthur's Seat, he created two villages which eventually became a town and later a city.

Legend has it that the pious David, hunting on a Sunday (not perhaps as heinous a crime then as it would have seemed after the Reformation!) was attacked and unseated by a stag at Holyrood. His life was saved only by grasping at a cross that had suddenly appeared between the stag's antlers and holding it up in a plea for Divine mercy. He founded the Abbey in gratitude for his delivery and an antlered stag with a cross on its forehead is still the coat of arms of the Canongate.

In 1633 Charles I was crowned there and its ruined walls still stand beside the royal Palace of Holyroodhouse. It survived in one form or another until the abdication of James VII in 1688 when the Protestant mob ravaged it on hearing of William of Orange's arrival in London.

FEUDS AND ASSASSINATION
The two burghs of Canongate and Edinburgh linked together gave Scotland a capital city and, after the fierce and bitter War of Independence under Robert the Bruce, in 1329 the victorious Scottish king granted a new charter to Edinburgh which established the city's rights over the Port of Leith.

The reigns of the early Stuarts, Bruce's successors as kings in the 15th century through his daughter, Marjory, were beset by feuds, battles and assassination and none of the first four Jameses died in bed.

JAMES I

The poetic James I was murdered in a tennis court in Perth. 'Fiery Face' James II was blown up by one of his great new cannons at Roxburgh Castle. The cultural dilettante, James III, was mysteriously murdered by a priest when fleeing from the Battle of Sauchieburn, and the flower of them all, the 'Renaissance Prince', James IV, died gallantly but uselessly on the field of Flodden.

Only James IV, who was 16, was other than a child when he came to the throne, and the whole history of the Stuarts up to James VI of Scotland and I of England is bedevilled by regencies and squabbles among ambitious and self-seeking guardians of the child monarchs.

When James IV came to the throne in 1488, Scotland seemed on the threshold of a new era. James had almost all the talents save one—discretion. He was handsome, accomplished in all the martial and social arts and a great many other things besides. He spoke eight languages, was skilled in medicine and gave Edinburgh a Royal College of Surgeons in 1506 and Scotland its first printing press in 1508. In 1496 he introduced the first compulsory Education Act.

High-spirited and lively, interested in everything from alchemy to music, he made Edinburgh into a city of European stature.

At the end of the Royal Mile, which leads down from the Castle to Holyrood, he built a splendid new palace to house his bride. This was to celebrate the union of the Thistle and the Rose—James IV of Scotland and Margaret Tudor, daughter of Henry VII of England.

There had been a building of some kind beside Holyrood Abbey before, for James II was born there, but the royal residence had been in the Castle. Until James made it into a palace for his English Queen, Holyrood was probably a royal guest house, used when there were ceremonies at the Abbey.

But Queen Margaret's brother, Henry VIII, when he

THE STORY OF EDINBURGH

succeeded to the English throne, was not content to have peace along the Border. The marriage treaty with Scotland was broken by resumed Border raiding and a golden age in Scotland came to a tragic end.

Partly because of the renewal of Border strife and partly in response to a plea from the Queen of France for help against Henry, who had renewed the English claim to the throne of Louis XII by invading France, James assembled his army on what is now the Meadows.

The Bore Stone set into the northern wall of Morningside Parish Church in Morningside Road is traditionally supposed to be that in which James set his standard before marching south into England and the greatest battle disaster in Scottish history.

At Flodden in the foothills of the Cheviots, in 1513, James died with 10,000 of his men and 13 earls in a desperately fought but badly mismanaged conflict.

Once more the king of Scotland was a child. James V was two years old when his father died with the flower of Scottish chivalry at Flodden.

MOURNING AND TERROR

Edinburgh, in mourning and in terror, started work on a new wall around the city to defend it from invasion—fragments of a wall can still be seen, particularly in the Vennel on the western boundary of George Heriot's School and in Castle Wynd which leads from the Grassmarket up to the Castle Esplanade.

The feared invasion did not take place because Henry made his peace with France. By a supreme irony, typical of these devious times, when the instigator of the tragedy of Flodden, Queen Anne of France, died in 1514, her husband Louis XII married James IV's sister-in-law, Henry VIII's sister, Mary. The wedding celebrations with a bride of 16 proved too much for the 53-year-old French king and he dropped dead on 1 January 1515!

The affairs of Scotland and its child monarch were handled by an uneasy regency under Queen Margaret for a few months but she sacrificed her right to rule by remarrying. When she married the Earl of Angus, the new king's second cousin, the Duke of Albany, was summoned from France to be regent.

However, when he returned to France two years later to negotiate a treaty, he was held prisoner by the new French king, François I. Back in Edinburgh, the great families fought and squabbled for supremacy. The battle

JAMES V   MARY OF GUISE

spilled out of the debating chambers into the streets of the capital. In 1520 it culminated in a bloody encounter between the Douglases and the Hamiltons up and down the Royal Mile and in and out of the wynds and vennels off it, which Edinburgh folk called 'The Cleansing of the Causeway.'

During this time the boy king was held prisoner in the Castle, but in 1528, at the age of 16, he escaped and joined his mother in Stirling, where she was about to marry yet again (Henry VIII was not the only much-married Tudor).

The almost forgotten boy king turned out to be a man of character, with much charm, when he chose to exert it, but also with a less endearing streak of ruthlessness.

When he went to Paris in 1536 to marry the daughter of the Duke of Vendôme, he so disliked the look of his bride-to-be that he refused to go through with the ceremony! Tactfully, François I offered him one of his own daughters, Madeline. But the gentle Madeline survived only two months of the Scottish climate and James negotiated another French marriage to Mary of Guise, the formidable lady who became the mother of Mary, Queen of Scots.

James died at Falkland in 1542, just after he had heard of the birth of his daughter. He was 31 and had been king for 29 years. Once again Scotland had an infant sovereign.

MARY AND MARRIAGE

Henry VIII tried to arrange a marriage with his son, Edward, and when the Scots refused he responded with 'The Rough Wooing', a series of bloody and destructive raids on lowland Scotland, and, in 1548, the six-year-old Scottish Queen was sent to France. There 10 years later she married the Dauphin who was to become François II.

François died after only 17 months on the throne and, in 1561, Mary returned to Scotland, a tall red-haired girl of 18 who was instantly plunged into civil and religious strife. Her arguments with the reformer, John Knox, are famous and even he allowed her a modicum of grudging admiration.

But all her marriages were disastrous. Lord Darnley, related to the royal houses of both Scotland and England, was a dissolute fop, murdered in mysterious circumstances. The Earl of Bothwell was a self-seeking bully, and that marriage caused riots and civil war.

Escaping from imprisonment in Loch Leven Castle, Mary lost her last battle at Langside near Glasgow and fled to England seeking asylum from her cousin, Queen Elizabeth. There she found none of the solace nor support she sought.

Imprisoned for 19 years and finally executed at Fotheringay in 1587 on a charge of treason to a queen to whom she had never owed allegiance, her colourful and tragic story has held the world's imagination ever since.

Mary's son by Darnley, James VI of Scotland, became King of England when Elizabeth died in 1603. His departure for England, where he was known as James I, effectively marked the end of Edinburgh as a royal capital. But although not independent, Scotland was to have its own Parliament for another 100 years.

FRENCH CONNECTION

Mary, Queen of Scots' links with France are remembered in certain aspects of Scottish cooking. A butcher will prepare you a *gigot* of lamb or pork which may be brought to the table on a *ashet* (*assiette*), while in certain parts of Scotland a gooseberry is still a *grozart*. Some old dialect words, such as *tassie* (spoon), *gout* (a taste) and *dejeune* (breakfast) were also once common.

MARY, QUEEN OF SCOTS

James's second son came to Scotland to be crowned Charles I. During the Civil War the Marquis of Montrose fought a brilliant campaign to support the king, and after Charles's execution, the Lord Protector Cromwell came north to campaign against Charles II's attempt to regain the throne.

The last time the Scottish crown jewels, now in Edinburgh Castle, were used in a coronation ceremony was in 1651, when Charles II was crowned in Scone, a decade before his English coronation.

LAST OF THE STUARTS

The last of the Stuart kings, James II of England and VII of Scotland, came to Edinburgh when he was Duke of York as the King's Commissioner. It was not a happy time in Scotland with the bloody moorland battles being fought out between the King's men and the Covenanters, and James, the fanatical, slightly deranged Catholic, was not the man to solve these problems.

But oddly enough his only monument in the city is a frivolous one. He played a golf match on Leith Links with a local shoemaker, John Paterstone, as his partner against two English noblemen. The winnings enabled Paterstone to build a house called Golfer's Land in the Canongate, and the plaque he placed on it, inscribed with the sound golfing motto 'Far and Sure' can still be seen in the Royal Mile today.

When James succeeded to the throne on his brother's death in 1685, he immediately began laying the foundations of his own destruction by repealing all the laws against Catholicism. In Edinburgh he refurbished the Chapel Royal at Holyrood for Catholic worship and installed a printing press, operated by Jesuit priests, in the palace at the foot of the Canongate.

When he fled to France after 'The Glorious Revolution' of 1688, the Edinburgh mob destroyed both.

From the Scottish Parliament, which met in 1689 to decide whether or not to accept William of Orange as king, grew the idea of closer ties with England. In the years of famine with which the 17th century ended in Scotland, arguments in favour of union with the prosperous English were revived.

Protests and riots all over Scotland greeted the proposals for the Union of the Parliaments—Daniel Defoe, author of *Robinson Crusoe*, who was spying for the English Government in Edinburgh, left a graphic account of these times—but the Union went through in 1707 and the Parliament of Scotland was no more.

PRINCE CHARLIE AND THE '45

Four Jacobite rebellions aimed at restoring the exiled Stuarts to the throne had their origins in Scotland and, in the last of them in 1745, Bonnie Prince Charlie and his Highlanders took Edinburgh and crushed a Hanoverian army sent against them under Sir John Cope at Prestonpans.

The Prince had his father proclaimed king at the Mercat Cross in a document which appointed himself as Prince Regent and promised religious freedom to Scotland and the abolition of the Act of Union 'which has

---

BITTER END

After being helped to reach the mainland by Flora Macdonald, Charles later escaped in a French ship. For the rest of his life he lived abroad, making plots to return to England which could never succeed. The gallant, 'bonnie' young hero of the 1745 rebellion died in Italy a bitter, disappointed and drunken old man.

THE STORY OF EDINBURGH 17

BONNIE PRINCE CHARLIE

reduced Scotland to being no more than an English province'.

After the Battle of Prestonpans, Prince Charlie behaved with great humanity, in stark contrast to the brutality of the Duke of Cumberland after Culloden, and sent to Edinburgh for surgeons to treat the wounded of both sides.

One of the surgeons was John Rattray, captain of the Company of Gentlemen Golfers (now the Honourable Company of Edinburgh Golfers, the oldest golf club in the world), whose subsequent career supremely illustrates the advantages of belonging to a good club!

Taken prisoner at Culloden, he was saved from the gallows by his fellow member, Duncan Forbes, Lord President of the Court of Session, the senior judge in Scotland.

Two decades after Culloden, a new spirit was abroad in Scotland. There was a feeling of optimism, of renewed national vigour and pride—at least in the Lowlands.

There were developments in industry, agriculture and trade and an astonishing flourishing of literature, philosophy and the arts. James Craig published his plan for the New Town and Edinburgh became a centre of not merely British but European significance.

A NEW AGE

In the latter half of the 18th century the Scottish Enlightenment marked an age when, suddenly, all human knowledge became accessible and there were men of genius everywhere to drink at its fountain.

The greatest of the Scottish philosophers, David Hume, was one of the first to live in the New Town, and a plaque in St Andrew Square marks the site of his house. The building of the New Town earned Edinburgh the description of 'the most exciting Georgian city in Britain'. An excellent example of early town-planning, it took the aristocrats and the top professional families of Edinburgh across the Nor' Loch to live in an elegant city of squares and crescents, beautifully proportioned classical buildings and green space. Nothing could have been a greater contrast to the packed, vibrant, semi-squalor of the Old Town.

Hume was only one of the protagonists of Edinburgh's 'Golden Age'. Painters like Ramsay, Nasmyth and Raeburn, poets such as Fergusson, the older Ramsay and

Burns, novelists like Walter Scott, geologists like James Hutton, and architects such as Robert Adam and his brothers rubbed shoulders with the men who were revolutionising surgery, political economy, engineering, physics and a host of other subjects.

To Edinburgh came men of learning and distinction, drawn by its fame and its beauty—Dr Johnson, Jean Jacques Rousseau, Benjamin Franklin, Bismarck, Chopin, Mendelssohn and Hans Andersen among them.

The writings of Johnson and his ebullient biographer, James Boswell, and the enthusiasm of Queen Victoria and Prince Albert for scenery north of the Border made Scotland a desirable destination just at the time when the advent of rail travel made it a possible one.

The railway was one of the benefits which the Industrial Revolution brought to Edinburgh in the 19th century. It ran past the foot of the Castle Rock where the Nor' Loch had been drained.

EDINBURGH CASTLE

EDINBURGH TODAY

At the beginning of the century the New Town was being completed. At its end some of the literary and philosophical glory had faded, but Edinburgh had become famous as a medical centre through Simpson's use of anaesthetics and Lister's work on antiseptics. Banking and insurance, printing and brewing were also part of Edinburgh's commercial spectrum.

The 20th century added electronics and light industry to the capital's portfolio, and with the creation of the Edinburgh Festival in 1947 a determined bid was made for cultural recognition again.

Edinburgh hosted the Commonwealth Games in 1970 and 1986, and the advent of the Festival has helped to make tourism a major industry. The increase in Edinburgh's status is reflected in its range of international contacts. The city is twinned with Dunedin, Florence, Munich, Nice, San Diego, Vancouver and the Chinese city of Xi'an.

Ultimately, however, Edinburgh's attraction is founded not on its associations but on itself. This is a city in which the vistas, the light and the ambience is constantly changing. Down its streets and through its vennels and wynds there are altering views from every corner—of the sea, the hills, a crenellation of towers and spires, a sweep of dramatic or elegant buildings.

Capital Buildings

In no other city in Britain can you see so dramatically contrasted the romantic glamour of a medieval burgh and the reasoned elegance of a Georgian town. In Edinburgh the two lie side by side, both now surrounded by a Victorian outgrowth that is grand in itself.

An excellent starting point would be Greyfriars Churchyard, at the west end of the Kirk. Here, on the site of one of Edinburgh's pre-Reformation monasteries, is the city's architectural growth encapsulated. North is the Castle and the ridge-town of the medieval burgh; south is the line of the Old Town wall. To the west is the huge and magnificent presence of Heriot's Hospital, William Wallace's Renaissance triumph, and east is the 1721 part of Greyfriars Church.

THE OLD TOWN

To really appreciate Edinburgh's architecture to the full, you have to walk. The Old Town is about a mile long, from Castle to Palace. Its oldest feature is its ground plan—the upper part best pictured as a fish's skeleton, a backbone of High Street and a fringe on either side of smaller bones—the wynds, closes and entries of our medieval town.

To get the feel of the character of these closes, walk into Riddle's Court (322–8 Lawnmarket) or venture a few yards down Old Fishmarket Close (188–90 High Street). The courtyard buildings in Riddle's Court (1590) provide a good lesson in the Scottish vernacular style of building, common from the 16th to the 18th centuries for the homes of ordinary (but not poor) people. Buildings are of rubble stone, 'harled' (roughcast) on the outside for weather-proofing; the layout of windows is unplanned, irregular and full of surprises.

Across the street from Riddle's Court is the high frontage of Gladstone's Land (c.1620). The site is medieval in scope—the population's housing demands were intense, so that the only answer was to build high and narrow, piling house upon house in a vertical street. You can go into the lower floors (National Trust for Scotland) and appreciate the character of a painted interior of the 17th century.

John Knox's House (c.1540) in the High Street and Huntly House (c.1570) in the Canongate sum up the inconsistencies of the period—the varied building materials, from timber and plaster through stone-rubble to ashlar—and the delightful urge to gain upper floor space by throwing floors forward like protruding jetties.

MEDIEVAL TO BAROQUE

But what of grander styles? You can find Romanesque and Gothic in Edinburgh but you have to look for it. St Margaret's Chapel in the Castle is 12th-century Romanesque, and the ruined west façade of Holyrood is about a century later taking us forward into very early Gothic in a magnificently composed frontispiece. High

---

DUNKERS

For over 300 years the ground between the Old Town and Princes Street was flooded by the Nor' Loch. This not only protected this side of the town from attack but was also a place of punishment. In 1562 a pillar and stool were erected 'for dowkeing of fornicatournis, for the suppressing of the said vice'.

Gothic of the 15th century is represented at its best (for Scotland) in the choir of St Giles, a finely grand arrangement of vaults and ribs and heraldry. But beyond these there are other treasures for the enthusiast: Duddingston Parish Church, a surviving village centre, has an excellent Norman structure and doorway, Corstorphine Church is a 15th-century collegiate foundation, and Restalrig Church (a map and a car are essential for this one) has a very fine hexagonal chapel of 1477 added by James III, ribbed and piered to make it a small masterpiece.

The best of architectural style in the Old Town is reserved for its public buildings. Visit Heriot's Hospital quadrangle (1628), off Lauriston Place, and admire the sculptural decoration (scenes of childhood and philanthropy) over the north portal. Enter (except on Mondays) the law-courts off Parliament Square to enjoy Scotland's grandest 17th-century interior—the Parliament Hall of 1632, a vast gathering place under a magnificent hammer-beam roof of Danish oak. Step across the High Street from here to look, at least from the outside, at the City Chambers of 1753, a dourly classical façade by John Adam.

By far the most important secular building in the Old Town is the Palace of Holyroodhouse, built in the 1670s by Sir William Bruce for King Charles II—who never came. Bruce's quadrangle, its ranges of rooms set above open arcades, is a model in correct use of the classical orders. Corinthian rises from Ionic upon a Doric lower floor and the whole is topped by a 'Scottish' frieze and a royally embellished pediment.

Bruce's interiors at Holyrood form a *Grand Appartement* which represents baroque at its richest interpretation in Scotland. The rooms are arranged in *enfilade*, and in the King's Bedroom they reach a pitch of perfection unrivalled in Scotland.

EAU BROTHER!

Beer has been brewed in the Canongate since the 12th century, when the monks of Holyrood Abbey discovered that the local water made excellent ale. Six centuries later, the Younger brothers set up breweries in the area.

THE CLASSICAL NEW TOWN

Edinburgh is proud of its New Towns. Taken together these Georgian developments from 1767 to about 1840 form the largest urban conservation area in Britain, and at the Conservation Centre, 13A Dundas Street, you will find excellent literature and displays on the New Towns.

The town planners who created all this were various. There was the relatively unknown James Craig, who pioneered it all in 1767 with a rigorously unadventurous gridiron that turns upon the St Andrew Square—George Street—Charlotte Square spine. Then came Robert Reid and William Sibbald, who added the second New Town in parallel and to the north, with spinal Great King Street linking Drummond Place with Royal Circus. From the 1820s, the third New Town, to the west, was conceived by James Gillespie Graham with the grandest of polygons, circles and semi-circles. Moray Place represents the peak of New Town grandiloquence.

Other town planners contributed beyond this triple core: W H Playfair in the Calton Hill terraces, and James Milne in the Stockbridge streets, formerly on Sir Henry Raeburn's estate. It may be impossible to explore all these but, for a quiet, discreet cameo of off-centre Georgian style, walk up James Milne's Saxe-Coburg

Street (1821) past his elegant little St Bernard's Church and round the Place at the top-end.

What of the individual buildings? There is an overriding New Town house style, uniformly fronted, with basement, three storeys and attic. Front doors are beautifully fanlighted, windows are precisely positioned and astragalled in panes four up and three across (though Victorian and later taste have often changed these). The street-level façade is 'rusticated' with channelled ashlar, and elegant railings guard the basements.

With the possible exception of 8 Queen Street by Robert Adam, you need not worry about individual architects; these houses were just the normal expectation of an urban gentleman and any one of a dozen skilled builders could do the job—at a price. The north side of Charlotte Square (1791), of course, is something different, for here—for the first time—a notable architect, Robert Adam, imposed his own wishes and his highly elaborate elevation upon whoever came to build on this street-terrace site. As a result this 11-house block is one of the triumphs of 18th-century informed taste.

ROBERT ADAM AND AFTER

Robert Adam was not much involved in domestic house building in Edinburgh, unlike his rival William Chambers who built Dundas House (1771—now the Royal Bank) in St Andrew Square, well worth two glances, and Duddingston House in the suburbs, sadly, scarcely worth one. His Edinburgh *métier* lay in his public buildings; notably, the circular monument to David Hume in the Calton Burial Ground, the massive Register House at Princes Street's east end, and the University on South Bridge. Register House (1774) is monumental, its plan as a repository for Scotland's records owing not a little to Robert Adam's memory of vast Roman baths.

The University's Old College was started by Robert Adam in 1789, and finished by W H Playfair about 1830. Playfair was the dominant figure in late Georgian and Victorian Edinburgh, and it is worth going in to the University's Art Centre, or to its Library Hall, to see how Adam's restrained classicism grows in magisterial character with Playfair under the influence of Victorian self-aggrandisement.

Playfair was Scotland's leading neo-Greek. On Princes Street his Royal Scottish Academy (built 1822–36) is a most enjoyable Greek Doric style. But for Playfair's Athens Revisited go up to the top of the Calton Hill and enjoy his classical collection.

NATIONAL MONUMENT ON CALTON HILL

VICTORIAN EDINBURGH

It is when you go out into the inner suburbs that Victorian taste runs riot. Edinburgh has always been a great place for schools and hospital-schools and—following the model of 17th-century Heriot's Hospital—a great anthology of these was achieved in the 19th century, each wilder than the next. You need a car to search these out but for sheer architectural extravaganza it is worth the effort. Playfair built the largest of them all—Donaldson's Hospital (1841) on the main road west from Haymarket. It is a sort of Hardwick Hall and

CAPITAL BUILDINGS

Burghley House rolled into one and might easily be mistaken by a *revenant* King Charles I for a Royal Palace; in fact it is a school for the deaf. The Orphan Hospital (1831, now Dean Education Centre) on Belford Road is neo-baroque by Thomas Hamilton, and it faces the neo-Greek Watson's Hospital (1825, now the Gallery of Modern Art) by William Burn. Hamilton and Burn were notable contemporaries and, at least in part, expert neo-classicists; Burn otherwise excelled in country houses. Finally, there are Daniel Stewart's Hospital (1848 by David Rhind) on Queensferry Road and Fettes College (1864 by David Bryce), visible half a mile to the north.

Edinburgh has nothing to match the *fin-de-siècle* advance into modern times pioneered in Glasgow by Charles Rennie Mackintosh, but his contemporary Sir Robert Lorimer (died 1929), who excelled in reviving the vanishing craftsmanship of architectural decoration, is represented by two outstanding buildings. One is the Thistle Chapel, the south-east appendage to St Giles added in 1910 and a triumph of High Gothic revival. The wood carving, metal work and tincturing show the achievement of Lorimer in creating an 'Edinburgh School of Craftsmanship', a salutary rival to the reputation of the 'Glasgow Boys'. Lorimer's other great building is on Edinburgh Castle, the immensely reverential, immensely moving national shrine to the memory of Scotland's recent fallen. In its steely, unbending restraint, classical in its dignity, it must surpass any other commemorative architect's creation.

MODERN TIMES

So finally to today! What can we encourage the visitor to enjoy among post-war additions to the Edinburgh scene? There are some you should not see (if you can help it): for ill-sited brutalism, the Grassmarket's Mountbatten Building, Holyrood Road's Moray House Gymnasium, and Leith Street's St James Centre take a lot of beating. In contrast, the newest Festival Square, facing the Usher Hall on Lothian Road will be glossy and painlessly acceptable when it is finally squared off. The Scottish Widows Fund building (1972) on Dalkeith Road is very exciting in its polygonal design, echoing the nearby basaltic polygons of Arthur's Seat. Indeed the Commonwealth Pool next door (1967) has a clean-cut presentation much to be admired. But praise in modern building activity in Edinburgh must also be given to the often small-scale in-fills that take place on Old Town sites. Off the Canongate or the High Street—as at Chessel's Court or, very recently, the Museum of Childhood building—new structures have appeared that are sensitive to scale and the vernacular tradition.

On the whole, Edinburgh's architectural inheritance is in good hands. The New Town Committee, the Old Town Committee, both armed with statutory teeth, and the powerful over all watchdog, the Cockburn Association, present an informed strength of opinion that it will take more than an ordinary developer to overcome.

But a heritage needs appreciation, and it is the awareness of value and the appreciation of merit by the visitor that will help Edinburgh to remain an architectural treasury of great worth.

SEEING STARS

Although it was founded back in the early 19th century, Edinburgh's Royal Observatory is kept right up to date. Today it is responsible for various national facilities including a 1.2m-aperture, wide-angle telescope in Australia, a 3.8m-aperture, infra-red telescope in Hawaii, and the COSMOS advanced measuring machine. Each of these facilities is the most powerful of its kind in the world.

The Royal Mile

*T*he hard, spiky spine of the Old Town, the Royal Mile is one of the most famous and historic thoroughfares in the world, where riots have spilled across the streets, clansmen battled and nobles duelled and rich and poor, obscure and famous, shared the cramped but lively democracy of life in tall tenements.

Much more than the lofty vistas of the New Town the Royal Mile retains the flavour of Scotland's ancient capital, once a settlement of gaunt tenements—Europe's first skyscrapers—some as high as 16 storeys. In the mid-18th century, about 50,000 people were crammed in the Royal Mile's tenements and in adjoining narrow streets, the rich on the upper floors for the best air, the poor on the lower ones.

Here, poets Robert Burns and Robert Fergusson drank with the literati in taverns and clubs, the poet, bookseller and wigmaker, Allan Ramsay, kept his shop and, among other lofty intellects, David Hume, philosopher and historian, and Adam Smith, author of *The Wealth of Nations*, lived.

1 Walkers, starting downwards, at Castlehill on the Esplanade are, because of a legal fiction by King Charles I (1625–49), standing on what was Nova Scotia soil. So as to create the orders of Knight-baronet of Scotland and Nova Scotia and because of the difficulties of carrying out the investiture ceremony in Nova Scotia, the King made the Esplanade part of the colony for that purpose. At the Esplanade entrance a plaque commemorates witch-burnings; more took place there than anywhere else in Scotland.

2 The first significant building is Cannon Ball House. It was once a merchant's house, dated 1630 and so named because the ball lodged in the west wall may have been fired from the castle at the Jacobite siege of 1745. More probably it marks the gravitation height of Edinburgh's first piped water supply to the area in 1681.

3 A diversion (*left*) down Ramsay Lane to Ramsay Gardens shows fantastic, turreted houses. The area was named after the poet, Allan Ramsay, who, about 1740, built an octagonal house, known to local wits as the 'Goose Pie'. His son, also named Allan, a portrait painter to King George III, erected more houses. At the end of the

24 THE ROYAL MILE

REFLECTED GLORY

Enter the viewing chamber of the Camera Obscura and you could be inside the body of a giant photographic camera. When the door closes, a live, moving image of Edinburgh is projected on to a circular white table in front of you. As the lens sweeps round on its panoramic tour of the city, a guide provides an informative commentary.

last century, Sir Patrick Geddes, the pioneering town planner who did much to rehabilitate the Royal Mile, remodelled buildings romantically to lure back university teachers and students to the Old Town.

4 Again at Castlehill is Boswell's Court, named after Dr John Boswell, the medical practitioner and uncle of James Boswell, Dr Johnson's biographer. The great lexicographer is said to have dined there with the two Boswells.

5 On the left is the castellated Outlook Tower with its Camera Obscura offering fascinating views of Edinburgh. The building's lower part is 17th century; the upper parts were added in 1853 when it was known as Short's Observatory. Near the end of the last century, Sir Patrick Geddes developed the building as a sociological museum when it was given its present name.

6 Further down is the Gothic Tolbooth St John's Church. Completed in 1844, it served, until recently, the city's Highland community. Its 241ft spire is the highest in Edinburgh.

7 At the Lawnmarket, once a bustling cross between a country fair and an Indian camp, is Upper Bow, the head of one of the Old Town's most characteristic winding streets, now mainly demolished. Here was the house of Major Thomas Weir, commander of the City Guard, a pious church member who, with his sister, Grizel, confessed to dealing in witchcraft. Both were strangled and burned in 1670, the Major's ghost on a headless black horse being reported in the area for many years afterwards.

8 Opposite, Mylne's Court and James' Court were attempts to bring fresh air into the area by demolishing old tenements and rebuilding others to form open squares. The first, built in 1690 by Robert Mylne, Master Mason to the King, is now a university hall of residence. The second, built in 1725 by James Brownhill, was described by the philosopher, David Hume, as 'very elegant but too small to display my great talent for cookery'.

9 A short way down the same side, Gladstone's Land, an older property acquired in 1617 by Thomas Gledstanes, an Edinburgh merchant and burgess, is the best-preserved example of a 17th-century house in the Old Town. Owned and renovated by the National Trust for Scotland, it is furnished in authentic 17th-century style.

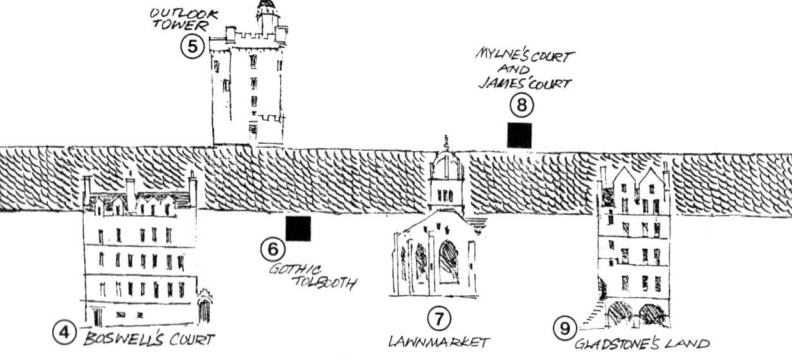

THE ROYAL MILE

10 Lady Stair's House (1622) became, early in the 18th century, the house of Eleanor, Countess of Stair. A hole under the fore-stair of the house once provided shelter for the family sow. The house is now a Robert Burns, Sir Walter Scott and Robert Louis Stevenson museum. In 1786 Burns lived in a house in the close.

11 Across the street is 16th-century Riddle's Court. Here Bailie MacMorran lived, one of the richest men in his time. He was shot dead in 1595 by High School boys as he tried to restore order during a pupils' riot over reduced holidays.

12 Further down is Brodie's Close, home of William Brodie, town councillor and Deacon of the Wrights, upright citizen by day but burglar by night to pay off gambling debts and support two mistresses and five illegitimate children. He was hanged on 1 October 1788 by a gibbet to which he had earlier made improvements. Brodie, the inspiration for Stevenson's *Dr Jekyll and Mr Hyde*, tried to cheat death by wearing an iron collar under his shirt, but failed.

13 At the intersection of George IV Bridge and Bank Street and into High Street are (*on the right*) three brass plates marking the city's last public hanging in 1864. William Burke, who with Hare sold to anatomists the bodies of people they murdered, was hanged there in 1828.

14 On the right is Parliament Square with Parliament House, built in 1639, where the Scottish Parliament and courts met until the Union of the Scottish and English Parliaments in 1707, and which now houses the High Court, Court of Session and Signet Library. The square, with the only representation of Charles II on horseback, was once 'the busiest and most populous nook of the old town'.

15 A heart-shaped pattern of setts in the west square marks the site of the Old Tolbooth. Demolished in 1817, it served for over 400 years as council chamber, courthouse, place of execution and tolls' collection. It is an Edinburgh custom to spit on the spot.

16 St Giles, the High Kirk of Edinburgh, with its superb crown tower, is the most dominant building in the Old Town. John Knox, the fiery verbal scourge of Mary, Queen of Scots, was appointed minister after the Reformation, and it was the scene of riot in 1637 when reforms, introduced by Charles I, were claimed to savour

GLOSSARY

Close an entrance to a tenement, also sometimes providing access to the rear of the building. There was often a gate at the front entrance which was closed at night

Court A courtyard surrounded on all sides by buildings

Land A tenement block of flats

Pend An archway

Vennel A lane or passageway

Wynd A thoroughfare, open from end to end.

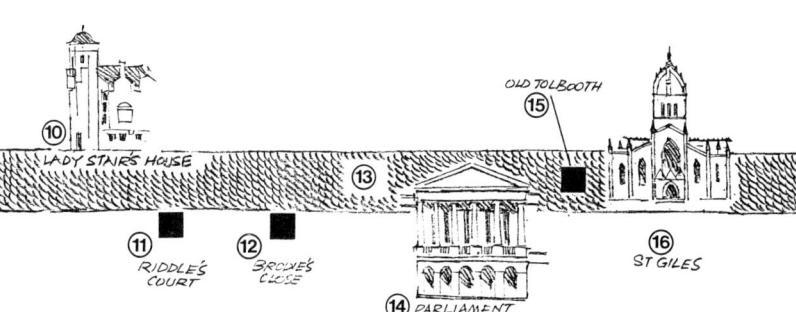

THE ROYAL MILE

of popery. Jenny Geddes, a vegetable seller, is said to have hurled a stool at the Bishop of Edinburgh who dared 'sing masse in my lugge' (ear).

17 On the opposite side is Advocates Close, one of the most picturesque of Edinburgh's alleyways and once so narrow that residents could almost shake hands with those opposite. Sir James Stewart, the Lord Advocate, lived there from 1692 to 1713.

18 A few yards down from St Giles, the Mercat Cross contains in its shaft part of the original 15th-century cross—its site marked nearby on the roadway—at which many famous Scots were executed. The present cross, erected in 1885, is still the scene of royal proclamations.

19 The neo-classical City Chambers opposite was completed in 1761 as the Royal Exchange. In 1811 it was used by the municipal authorities and later expanded; its 12-storey rear in Cockburn Street is one of the tallest surviving Old Town buildings. A wall plaque past the courtyard shows what was the entrance to Craig's Close, the site of the Cape Club, which numbered some of Edinburgh's most famous citizens among its membership, including the poet, Robert Fergusson. On the same side is Anchor Close, the meeting place of the Crochallan Fencibles, a club for 'men of original character and talent'. Burns was introduced to it in 1787 by his printer, William Smellie, whose premises were in the close and who printed the *Encyclopaedia Britannica's* first edition in 1768.

20 Across the street is the Old Assembly Close where fashionable balls were held in the Old Assembly Rooms; Oliver Goldsmith remarked on the gaiety of them and the beauty of the girls there. A few yards down is New Assembly Close, where dancing assemblies were also held; it is now the site of the Wax Museum.

21 The elegant Countess of Eglinton—to whom Allan Ramsay dedicated his pastoral drama, *The Gentle Shepherd*—and her seven beautiful daughters, whose procession of sedan chairs to dancing assemblies always drew crowds, lived opposite at Old Stamp Close. Here Flora Macdonald, who saved Prince Charlie from the pursuing government troops, went to school.

PIPED PLONK

Mercat Cross was a place of public proclamation. At Charles II's proclamation in 1661, workmen were told to prepare 'upon the crosse pyps of leid and such other things necessary for running of wyne at the spoutts and to provide wyne glasses for the said use'. Royal proclamations are still made from the cross, but the 'wyne' is long gone.

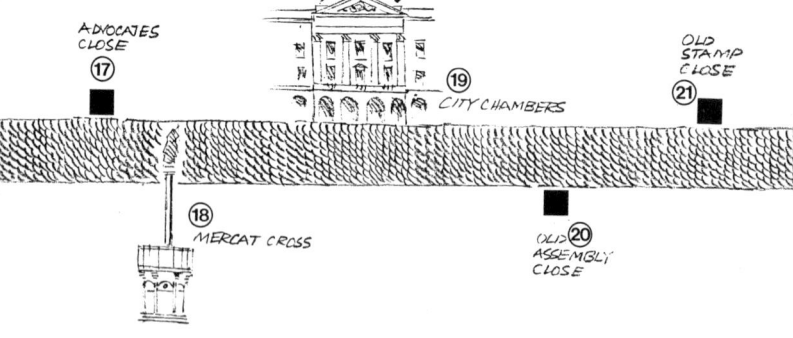

22 On the right is the Tron Kirk, named after a nearby public weigh beam or *tron*. Completed around 1648, its original wooden steeple stood until 1824 when its destruction by fire was like a 'beautiful firework'. The fine hammer-beam roof survived and a new stone spire was built in 1828. Here, Edinburgh traditionally celebrates the New Year. The church was closed in 1952.

23 Crossing the North Bridge and South Bridge intersection on the left is Carrubber's Close, once a Jacobites' haunt. John Spottiswood, Archbishop of St Andrews and Scots historian (1565–1639), who crowned Charles I at Holyrood in 1633, lived here. Allan Ramsay had a shop and opened a theatre here in 1736 but closed it after puritanical magistrates refused a licence.

24 Further down are Bailie Fyfe's Close and Paisley Close. In 1861 a tenement between them collapsed, killing 35 occupants. Rescuers found a trapped boy who shouted, 'Heave awa' chaps. I'm no deid yet'. The incident is commemorated by a sculpture of the boy's face and an inscription.

25 On the other side is the Museum of Childhood, an imaginative collection of old and new toys.

26 Moubray House (*left*) was where Daniel Defoe, author of *Robinson Crusoe* and suspected English spy, lived and edited the *Edinburgh Courant* in 1710. This is one of the oldest city houses, dated perhaps 1462, with characteristic outside stair, and was once a tavern; now it is a private house.

27 Nearby is John Knox's House, one of the oldest (about 1490) and most distinctive buildings in the Old Town. The preacher is believed to have occupied it between 1561 and 1572, though perhaps only for three months. In 1571 a musket was fired through a window, the ball lodging in the ceiling of the room in which he sat. The house was earlier owned in 1556 by James Mossman, goldsmith to Mary, Queen of Scots, and his wife, Mariota Arres.

28 Opposite is Hyndford's Close, where Jean Maxwell lived, wife of Alexander, Duke of Gordon (1743–1827). A beauty and leader of fashion, Scott said her 'sole claim to wit rested upon her brazen impudence and disregard to the feelings of all who were near her'.

29 On the same side is Tweeddale Court, once the mansion of Dame Margaret Kerr, wife of the 7th Lord Hay of Yester. It became the British Linen Bank's head office, and, in a famous murder, a bank porter, William Begbie,

ONE FOR THE ROAD

Recent excavations inside Tron Kirk revealed the cobbled surface of a thoroughfare. This was called Marlin's Wynd after the Frenchman, Jean Marlin, who first paved the High Street. When he died, Marlin was buried in the middle of the street, as an honour.

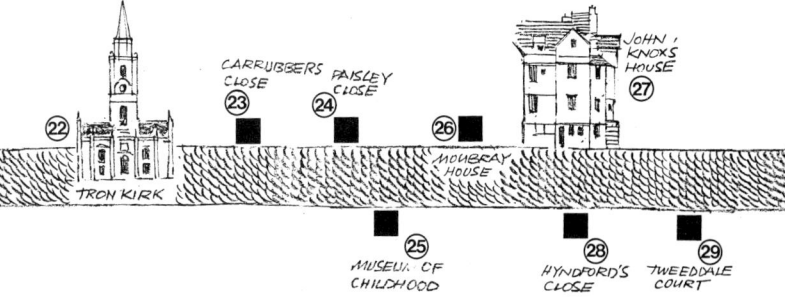

28 THE ROYAL MILE

was stabbed to death there in 1806 by an unknown person and robbed of £4,392. In 1817, the bank was succeeded by Oliver & Boyd publishers, who occupied it until 1973. The Scottish Poetry Library is here.

30 Lower right is World's End Close, the last close before the old city wall and the outside world—in this case the Canongate, meaning the way of the monks walking to Edinburgh from Holyrood Abbey. Once highly fashionable, in 1769 it could still boast among its residents: 2 dukes, 16 earls, 7 barons, 7 judges and 13 baronets.

31 Moray House (*right*), built in 1628, now a teacher training college, was owned by the Earls of Moray and famed for its elegant gardens. Charles I visited it and Cromwell made it his headquarters in 1648. The Treaty of Union was signed here by the 'parcel of rogues'.

32 Downwards, on the same side is Huntly House, a fine 1570 dwelling, once the home of the Dowager Countess of Gordon, and now the city museum.

33 Bakehouse Close, nearby, is a favourite of artists, and richly evokes the atmosphere of the Old Town.

34 Adjoining, Acheson House is a superb example of a 17th-century baronial town house and now the Scottish Craft Centre.

35 On the left is the 1591 Scoto-French-style Canongate Tolbooth. Formerly a council chamber, courthouse, jail and collection place for burgh dues, it is now a museum.

36 Further down is the Canongate Church, built in 1688. English soldiers taken prisoner by Prince Charlie's army after his victory at Prestonpans were held there. Those buried in the churchyard include the poet, Robert Fergusson, Mrs Agnes McLehose and Burns's 'Clarinda'.

37 Still descending, one sees Whitefoord House (*left*), which takes its name from Sir John Whitefoord (died 1803), now a veterans' residence.

38 Opposite is Queensberry House, where the 2nd Duke of Queensberry accepted a bribe of £12,325 to push through the Treaty of Union. It is now an old people's hospital.

39 Left is White Horse Close, a 1964 restoration of 17th-century houses and coaching inn, the last said to be the quarters for Prince Charlie's officers during his 1745 occupation of the city.

40 Then comes Abbey Strand and the walk ends at the gates leading to Holyrood Palace. The distance from the drawbridge at Edinburgh Castle to the door of Holyrood Palace is 1 mile 106yd.

CANONGATE·TOLBOOTH

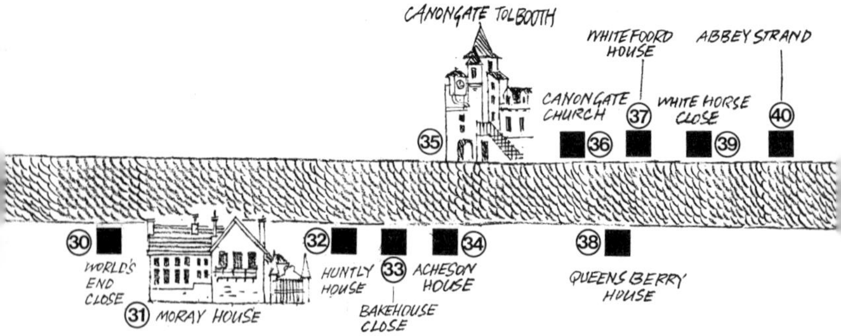

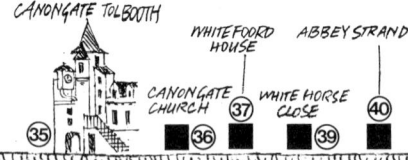

Edinburgh's Villages

*A*s cities expand, they tend to engulf existing communities. Dozens of villages have been swamped in the Scottish capital's development from an overcrowded community in the protective shelter of the Castle to the modern metropolis of Greater Edinburgh, which now covers an area of 51 square miles. In many cases, only traces of the original villages remain: in others, they survive as places with a character and an identity of their own.

CRAMOND

The picturesque village of Cramond, at the mouth of the River Almond, is one of the most popular spots for visitors, with its trim old white houses and quaint little courtyards off an alley running at right angles to the river. Equally trim and welcoming is the nearby hostelry, Cramond Inn, which dates from 1670.

There are few obvious signs that Cramond in the 18th century was the hub of a busy industrial area, not only milling grain—which it had done from at least 1178—but processing cloth, producing paper and pioneering in iron manufacture.

Very much earlier—about AD142—the Romans established a fort at Cramond, part of which has been excavated to the north of Cramond Kirk. A plan of the fort can be found adjacent to the church, which has medieval origins. The oldest part of the present church is its 15th-century tower.

Cramond Tower, a medieval stronghold, has been comprehensively restored. Between the tower and the churchyard is another historic building, Cramond House, which dates from 1680. Once the home of the Inglis family, lairds for generations, it is now owned by Cramond Kirk and used in part by the National Trust for Scotland.

Following the Almond inland from its estuary is the River Almond Walkway which leads to the remains of Fair-a-Far Mill and its weir.

A small ferryboat makes the short crossing of the River Almond to provide a pleasant walk in the grounds of Lord Rosebery's Dalmeny estate to Queensferry.

In the summer, exhibitions are mounted by the Cramond Heritage Trust in the Old Maltings.

COLINTON

Colinton, on the southern outskirts of the city, is today one of the most prosperous suburbs. It became a busy little place when the waters that tumbled through the beautiful wooded Colinton Dell were harnessed to turn the wheels of grain, flax, paper and snuff mills.

At the heart of village life was Colinton Parish Church. The present church, which dates from 1771 (though substantially altered since), is the successor to the Kirk of the Hailes, mentioned as early as 1097.

Charity was a strong tradition in Colinton. One

JUST A FORT

Cramond was the site of a 2nd-century Roman fort and takes its name from *Caeravon*—the fort on the river.

CHAIR LIFT

Horse-drawn carriages were of little use as transport in the steep and narrow closes of Edinburgh's Old Town. Sedan chairs, only 3ft wide and carried by two men, overcame this problem. They were introduced in the late 17th century and could be hired, like taxis, for standard fares between stances. Sedan chairs were also used as ambulances.

TREASURE GARDEN

Colinton church, its manse and garden, have strong links with Robert Louis Stevenson. His maternal grandfather, the Rev Dr Lewis Balfour, was the parish minister from 1823 to 1860 and Stevenson spent many childhood days excercising his vivid imagination in the garden and around the mills.

notable benefactor was James Gillespie of Spylaw, who owned a nearby snuff mill and made a fortune from it. He founded a hospital bearing his name, also a free school for the education of poor boys. Gillespie's mausoleum is in the churchyard.

The 19th century brought big changes to Colinton—a decline of the mills as steam power ousted water power, but an influx of new residents as a branch line of the Caledonian Railway brought the village within commuting range of Edinburgh. Many handsome villas were built, their architects including Sir Robert Lorimer.

Among historic buildings in the Colinton area are Colinton Castle (built 1450), now a ruin in the grounds of Merchiston Castle School, and the Covenanters' Monument in Redford Road.

DEAN VILLAGE

In complete contrast to the formal layout and classical order of the New Town is Dean Village, only five minutes or so from the west end of Princes Street. Before Thomas Telford's mighty Dean Bridge opened an easier road to Queensferry and the north, the route lay through one of the oldest villages in the city with milling associations dating back to the 12th century. Now known as Dean Village, it is entered by the steep Bell's Brae.

For centuries it was the domain of millers and bakers. The Incorporation of Baxters (bakers), a powerful Edinburgh guild, at one time operated 11 watermills and two granaries in the area. They have left their marks for the observant to spot. At the head of Bell's Brae is Kirkbrae House, on one side of which is a sculptured panel bearing symbols of the bakers' art, wheatsheafs and a ripening sun; also the inscription, from Genesis: 'In the sweat of thy face shalt thou eat bread', and the date 1619. It is believed to have come from a group of old mill buildings called Jerico, which stood in nearby Miller Row.

At the foot of Bell's Brae is a 17th-century building, a former meeting place of the baxters, with more craft symbols including crossed peels (bread shovels) and the crumbling inscription: 'God bless the Baxters of Edinburgh who built this House in 1675'.

The Incorporation of Weavers was also active in the village in the early 18th century. As milling and weaving declined, a number of tanneries came into prominence. Other local industries included distilling and brewing.

Today, much of Dean Village is residential and if it lacks the bustle of industry and even the shops which add life to an area, its situation in picturesque surroundings so near the heart of the city makes it a popular place to live.

Hawthorn Buildings, half-timbered on the upper floor and with walls of yellow ochre, is one example of imaginative 19th-century housing. Another is Well Court, built in 1884 by John R Findlay, proprietor of *The Scotsman*.

Much of Dean Village's charm is due to the rugged topography, the green banks of the Water of Leith, and the soaring arches of Telford's bridge.

STOCKBRIDGE

If the disappearance of Dean Village's shops robbed it of a true village atmosphere, that is not the case with its downstream neighbour, Stockbridge, a rural hamlet until the 18th century.

Stockbridge has been the spawning ground of writers, historians and artists, the most famous of whom was the portrait painter, Sir Henry Raeburn, born in 1756. A poor boy, orphaned at the age of six, he won fame and fortune from his painting, returning to the area to occupy St Bernard's, the principal mansion in old Stockbridge. From about 1813 he developed his own estate with property centred around the elegant Ann Street, named after his wife.

David Roberts, another prominent Stockbridge painter, born in 1796, became, like Raeburn, a Royal Academician. He lived at 17th-century Duncan's Land in Church Street, now a restaurant of character.

Notable buildings around Stockbridge include Playfair's St Stephen's Church and, in Henderson Row, the original Edinburgh Academy building opened in 1824. Adjacent is a former school for deaf children. This was taken over in 1977 by Edinburgh Academy but some years earlier featured as the fictional 'Marcia Blane School for Girls' in the 20th Century Fox classic film of Edinburgh attitudes and school life, *The Prime of Miss Jean Brodie*.

ST STEPHEN'S CHURCH

One of Stockbridge's more interesting housing developments is known as 'The Colonies'. It was constructed around 1861 by an Edinburgh building co-operative to provide low-cost housing for artisans.

LEITH

Though Leith—which for centuries was Scotland's chief port—has been part of Greater Edinburgh since 1920 and from medieval times has rarely been free of the capital's control, it is the only district of the city where the inhabitants talk about 'going to Edinburgh' when they make the 1½-mile journey to the city centre. It has always had a strong sense of local identity.

The original port of Leith grew up around the Shore, where the Water of Leith joins the River Forth. Early trade included the export of salt fish and hides and the import of wine from Bordeaux. A flourishing ship-building industry grew up. The *Sirius*, launched in 1837, was the first steamship to cross the Atlantic.

The industrial revolution brought new industries to Leith, including sugar-refining and glass-making. To cope with increased trade and bigger vessels, a succession of new docks was built—Victoria (1851), Albert (1869), Edinburgh (1881) and Imperial (1903).

The population expanded rapidly but the depression which followed World War I and industrial decline after World War II made Leith an unemployment black spot. A lot of post-war housing was unimaginative to say the least. Nevertheless, much of interest remains in Leith and there are signs of a distinct upturn in its fortunes. The 200-year-old commercial area of Constitution Street and Bernard Street is unique and has been spruced up. Sympathetic restoration of historic buildings in the area includes Andrew Lamb's House in Burgess Street, a fine example of a prosperous merchant's house of the early 17th century, and the early 18th-century King's Wark, which takes its name from a much older building on the site, established in the 15th century by James I of Scotland for handling ordnance and cargoes for Royal use.

Also in the historic Shore area is an attractive modern housing development called King's Landing which successfully echoes features of older Scottish domestic architecture. 'King's Landing' commemorates the fact that George IV made a ceremonious landing at the old port when he visited Edinburgh in 1822 (quite an event since he was the first British monarch to visit Scotland for over 100 years). Leith had had many earlier Royal visitors including the young Mary, Queen of Scots when she landed there to take the Scottish throne.

Leith Links, round which are some of Leith's better houses, has notable connections with archery and golf. Though there is no golf course there now, it was a popular game at the Links for centuries.

NEWHAVEN

The fishing village of Newhaven, just a mile west of Leith, enjoyed a brief period of glory in the 16th century when James IV, at war with England, had ambitions to build up a strong Scottish navy. Because of its deep water, Newhaven was chosen as the site of a new shipyard where a number of vessels were built, the most remarkable being the *Great Michael*, launched in 1511 as the Scottish flagship.

Newhaven reverted to its role of fishing village after the Battle of Flodden, where James IV was killed and Scotland's naval ambitions were abandoned. Apart from fish, there were massive oyster beds in the Firth of Forth and Newhaven enjoyed a monopoly in supplying oysters to the city of Edinburgh. These were immensely popular in the 18th and early 19th centuries but over-fishing eventually destroyed the beds. Herring were often abundant and, until quite recent times, Newhaven 'fishwives' were commonly seen in Edinburgh streets.

The flavour of old Newhaven remains, for fisherfolk's cottages have either been restored or replaced by cottages which retain traditional features.

The Peacock Hotel, a hostelry established by an 18th-century wine merchant, preserves much of the Newhaven traditions—in food, photographs and artefacts.

DUDDINGSTON

Close to the bird sanctuary of Duddingston Loch in Holyrood Park is Duddingston village, part of the new, quite extensive, suburban district of Duddingston. The 12th-century Duddingston Kirk stands near the park entrance.

Parallel with busy Old Church Lane, in a street called The Causeway, stands a former tavern where Bonnie Prince Charlie resided before his victory at the Battle of Prestonpans in 1745. From a state of dereliction this building has been restored as a private house by Duddingston Preservation Society. The Causeway is relatively quiet and secluded and Duddingston today exudes an orderly prosperity it did not know in the past. Apart from farm work, coal-heaving and flax-weaving were the mainstays of the village.

PARKING IN NEWHAVEN

Starbank Park is an ideal place to sit or stroll on a summer afternoon or evening. Its grassy slopes, bordered by beautiful flowers, overlook the Firth of Forth.

Duddingston has an ancient pub, the Sheep's Heid Inn, with origins in the 14th century, though the present building is only about 200 years old. The inn has the oldest skittle alley in Scotland, used for decades by the Trotters' Club, founded by Edinburgh journalists.

The 'roarin game' of curling has been played in Edinburgh for a very long time but its most popular venue in the late 18th and much of the 19th centuries was Duddington Loch.

CORSTORPHINE

The old village of Corstorphine, in what is now one of the largest districts of the city, grew up around 14th-century Corstorphine Castle, stronghold of the Forrester family. Nothing remains of the castle, but its beehive-shaped dovecote with nests for over 1,000 birds (winter food for the laird) is intact.

Corstorphine Kirk with its distinctive stone-slabbed roof has an unusual square tower dating from the early 15th century. Church-goers were directed to worship not only by a bell but by a beacon light on the east gable, in regular use from 1429 until 1769.

A very old sycamore tree near the dovecote was the scene of a violent quarrel one night in 1679 between a former Lord Forrester and his paramour, Christian Nimmo, who drew the sword from her lover's scabbard and ran him through. For his murder she was executed in Edinburgh two months later. The tree still stands, the subject of inevitable ghost stories.

In the mid-18th century Corstorphine was famous for its Physic Well, at the east end of the village. The site is marked by a number of flat stones in a wood near Dunsmuir Court.

SWANSTON

Few thatched cottages survive in Scotland but an attractive group that constituted the original village of Swanston, in the foothills of the Pentland Hills, was restored in the late 1950s.

By a gate from the village on to the hills is a seat commemorating the distinguished poet, Edwin Muir (1887–1959), who loved the spot. So, as a young man, did Robert Louis Stevenson, whose summer home from 1867 to 1880 was the handsome bow-windowed Swanston Cottage, about a quarter of a mile away. Notebook and pencil in hand, the teenage RLS questioned and cultivated the villagers, making a special friend of John Tod, the 'roaring' shepherd. Swanston Cottage and its environs feature in *St Ives*, in *Picturesque Notes* and the poem *Ille Terrarum*. The Pentlands, his *Hills of Home*, he remembered with nostalgia and wrote about from far-off Samoa, where he died.

The newer part of Swanston dates from around 1900 when farming was labour-intensive. Between the visitors' car park and the village is the historic farmhouse. In the 17th century it was a house of refuge for the Covenanters who fought the efforts of the Stuart monarchs to establish an Episcopalian form of church government in Scotland. Substantially rebuilt in the 18th century, Swanston farmhouse has now been converted into flats and has some modern additions.

The Festival & the Arts

When the Edinburgh Festival began in 1947 it was a gesture of cultural defiance in a world made weary by war, misery and destruction.

Britain was still in a period of belt-tightening austerity, food was rationed and one of my most vivid memories of the first Festival is conducting famished and bemused opera singers from countries which were supposed to have lost the war, to Edinburgh's best black market restaurants.

Quite a number of the sedate citizens of Edinburgh—and elsewhere—thought that the City Fathers of Scotland's capital were quite mad to have got themselves involved in the expense and complexity of producing the world's leading international arts festival in such parlous times.

But from the first there was nothing small-minded or penny-pinching about the Festival idea. If there was to be a Festival in the magnificent setting of Edinburgh, then it had to be planned and run on a scale worthy of the city itself.

The world of the arts in the largest sense was the source of Edinburgh programmes and has remained so. Nothing which impinges on the imaginative and creative element in man has been ignored.

ALL THE ARTS

Edinburgh is an across-the-board Festival, happily and generously embracing all the arts.

It is almost impossible to name a great contemporary orchestra, artist, theatre or dance company which has not appeared in Edinburgh at Festival time. August in Edinburgh is the time when you wonder what the rest of the world is doing—because everyone who matters seems to be here.

Mark you, the canny burghers of Scotland's capital did not arrive at this state of cultural euphoria in one easy leap. They were as dazed as anyone at what happened in the city in that splendid summer of 1947.

The first Festival took place in brilliant sunshine and

Italian opera singers brought up on generations of gloomy, weather-torn sets for Donizetti's *Lucia di Lammermoor* sweltered in Princes Street Gardens and swore blind that whatever might be the Scottish capital's Athenian pretensions, Edinburgh was definitely the Naples of the North.

Even after the clamorous success of the first Festival, Edinburgh citizens were not too sure about it. 'It couldn't have been us that did it,' they smirked at one another. 'It must have been a fluke.'

And, in a sense, they were right enough. The impetus for the Festival came largely from outside.

MAJOR FESTIVAL FOR BRITAIN

Rudolf Bing, then the manager of Glyndebourne Opera, wanted to create a major festival in Britain while the only two arts festivals in the world which counted for anything, Salzburg and Bayreuth were struggling to raise themselves like phoenixes from the shattered and smouldering ruins of the Third Reich. It was an act of calculated cultural banditry. Bing did not care where the festival was to be held. He tried first for Oxford and Cambridge, both convenient to the pool of culture enthusiasts centred in London and the home counties.

Edinburgh only came into his calculations when the great university cities of England showed little interest and when the persuasions of Audrey Christie, wife of Glyndebourne's founder, and H Harvey Wood, the British Council's man in Scotland, had advocated to him the virtues of the Scottish city.

Later Harvey Wood assembled some impressive, influential and persuasive Scottish patrons—among them Lady Rosebery, Lord Cameron and Sir Andrew Murray—to back the Festival idea and sell it to Edinburgh. Thanks to their support, the Lord Provost, Sir John Falconer, eloquently managed to persuade the City Fathers to vote money to set the Festival on its way.

Having no local composer—as Bayreuth has Wagner and Salzburg Mozart—around whom to build its festival, Edinburgh decided from the outset to 'go for broke', as the Americans say.

PATTERN SET

In that first year of 1947, the operas *Le Nozze di Figaro* by Mozart and Verdi's *Macbeth* were given at the King's Theatre. At the Usher Hall there was the Vienna Philharmonic, reunited with Bruno Walter for the first time since he had been driven from Austria by Nazi persecution in 1937, and the Orchestre des Concerts Colonne from Paris.

There was also the Hallé under Barbirolli, the Liverpool Philharmonic under Sargent, the Scottish Orchestra under Susskind, the BBC Scottish Orchestra conducted by Ian Whyte and one of the most magical string quartets ever assembled, Schnabel, Szigeti, Fournier and Primrose.

At the Lyceum Theatre Louis Jouvet from Paris was playing Moliere's *L'École des Femmes* and Giraudoux's *Ondine* with Dominique Blanchar. The Old Vic staged *The Taming of the Shrew* with such well known names as Trevor Howard, Bernard Miles and Patricia Burke and

THE FESTIVAL & THE ARTS

LONG FRINGE

The only trouble with the Fringe is that by the time you have finished reading the massive programme, it is almost too late to go to anything! There can be up to 1000 titles, offered by 500 different companies, plus exhibitions, 'happenings' and all kinds of music from pop to Stockhausen.

Alec Guinness's interpretation of *Richard II*.

At the Empire (now a bingo hall) Margot Fonteyn danced Tchaikovsky's *Sleeping Beauty* above the baton of Constant Lambert. At the Freemason's Hall there were morning chamber music concerts and recitals.

Other events such as exhibitions of painting and sculpture, the Tattoo and the enormous artistic splurge that is the Fringe were added later, but the basic Festival pattern as it is today was established in 1947—opera, concerts, chamber music, English and foreign language theatre and dance. The make-up and balance of the programme has varied with the tastes and interests of successive directors.

Bing departed after two years to be General Manager of the Metropolitan Opera in New York and he was succeeded by his 30-year-old assistant, Ian Hunter, a remarkable young man who had been a Lieutenant-Colonel during the war and created an opera company in occupied Austria.

Hunter added major art exhibitions—some of the greatest seen anywhere—and enlarged the opera spectrum by inviting foreign companies to perform.

Hunter left in 1956 and his successor, Robert Ponsonby, continued the interest in the visual arts with memorable exhibitions of Braque and Monet, opera from La Scala, Milan, and also some dazzling theatre from Italy directed by Giorgio Strehler. Among the ingredients Ponsonby introduced was satire—Anna Russell making fun of the Festival; Flanders and Swan pricking pomposities and, most famous of all, *Beyond the Fringe* which introduced Dudley Moore, Peter Cook, Alan Bennett and Jonathan Miller to an appreciative world.

The Fringe itself was growing fast. In numbers of performances it had already outstripped the 'official' Festival. It included everything from biting satire, through one-man or woman shows to performances of the classics and chamber music.

These performances received no official financial backing and they were presented by amateurs, young professionals, university students and groups determined to make a name for themselves.

CULTIVATED INDISCIPLINE

The quality varied widely, as it still does today. The hectic, cultivated indiscipline of the Fringe regularly throws up performances of genius and tremendous talent and commitment and, just as regularly, rubbish and everything in between.

At Festival time, Fringe Festival, Film Festival, Jazz Festival, Book Festival and so on are presenting something like 300 performances a day. It is impossible to have a dull time in Edinburgh during the Festival.

There have been some stunningly memorable performances in the last 40 years. Kathleen Ferrier's *Das Lied von der Erde*, with Bruno Walter; the rumbustious exuberance of the old Scots classic *The Thrie Estaites*; T S Eliot's *The Cocktail Party*; Jean-Louis Barrault's *Hamlet* in French; a great Verdi *Requiem* from the orchestra of La Scala; another *Hamlet* from Richard Burton and Claire Bloom; Maria Callas's *La Sonnambula* in the first decade.

When he became Director in 1961 Lord Harewood

presented a superb performance of Schoenberg's *Gurrelieder* and featured particular composers in each year, notably Russians like Shostakovitch and Indian artists. Peter Diamand, the longest serving Festival Director, continued this plan and put the emphasis firmly back on great opera performances, culminating in a magnificent *Carmen* with Berganza and Domingo, dazzlingly conducted by Claudio Abbado.

John Drummond, when he took over from Diamand in 1978, took another direction with more ballet performances, exhibitions and Russian drama.

Frank Dunlop, who took over in 1984, has mounted spectacular, wide-ranging world theatre with companies from Japan to Scandinavia.

The list of innovative and memorable performances threatens to stretch out, like Macbeth's line of kings 'to the crack of doom'.

And that is without taking account of the Fringe, which has grown more and more professional down the years, the Film Festival, the Jazz Festival, the Tattoo and many other events of these three hectic summer weeks!

There was a time when it was widely held that after the Festival the arts in Edinburgh died for 49 weeks. It was never true and today it is less true than ever.

Music is provided by regular concerts from the Scottish National Orchestra, the Scottish Chamber Orchestra, the Scottish Baroque Ensemble, the Edinburgh Quartet and visiting groups and artists.

There is a very talented resident company at the Royal Lyceum Theatre and the Traverse in the Grassmarket remains a British leader in presenting new and avant-garde plays.

The City's fine museums and art galleries, the National Gallery, Royal Scottish Academy, the City Art Centre, the Scottish Gallery of Modern Art, Richard de Marco's new gallery in Blackfriars Street and the Fruitmarket Gallery offer constantly changing and challenging views of the visual arts.

There is folk music, rock and jazz in pubs, chamber music and recitals in the New Town and elsewhere throughout the year.

The arts flourish in Edinburgh all the year round. The Festival is simply the brilliant firework display which is the peak of the arts year in the capital of Scotland.

EDINBURGH TATTOO

Famous Residents

To be a hero or a character in Edinburgh your deeds or your eccentricities should be on a very large scale, otherwise they stand in serious danger of being dwarfed by the city's dimensions and landscape.

Yet that does not seem to have been a danger in the 18th-century days of Mr Amyat, King George's chemist:

> Here I stand at what is called the cross of Edinburgh and can in a few minutes take 50 men of genius by the hand. . . . In Edinburgh the access to men of parts is not only easy but their conversation and the communication of their knowledge are at once imparted to intelligent strangers with the utmost liberality.

But there were characters in Edinburgh before Mr Amyat trod its streets, deemed heroes by some if less highly regarded by others.

JOHN KNOX—PROTESTANT REFORMER

One who was only too prepared to communicate his knowledge was John Knox, the famous Protestant reformer, challenger of Mary, Queen of Scots on her return to Scotland from France. Actually, it was Mary who challenged Knox.

She had returned to Scotland on the understanding that everyone should be allowed to practise religion in their own way. When she had mass said in the Chapel Royal, Knox thundered denunciation of her from the pulpit of St Giles High Kirk.

Mary summoned him to the Palace of Holyroodhouse, accusing him of treason and of insulting herself and her mother in writing his *First Blast of the Trumpet Against the Monstrous Regiment of Women*, published in 1558, in which he had asserted that the rule of women was 'the subversion of good order, of all equity and justice'.

In 1548 Knox had been captured at St Andrews Castle by the French and had spent two years as a galley slave on their ships, so he had no liking for French ways, which he associated with Mary. Knox brought to Scotland the austere doctrines of John Calvin with whom he had worked in Geneva. To a large degree his teachings set the pattern for Scottish religious and even social life over the next few centuries, not all of it harsh and over-moralistic, for it included wide-reaching provisions for democratic rule by elections and compulsory education.

GOLD DIGGER AND MATHEMATICIAN—JOHN NAPIER

Born in Knox's lifetime in 1550 was John Napier of Merchiston, an Edinburgh man of very different stamp, son of the Master of the Scottish Mint who discovered gold in the Pentland Hills. He shared Knox's Presbyterian views but it was in the field of mathematics, astronomy and invention that he excelled.

Napier's supreme achievement was the invention of logarithms and the decimal point, which led the way

JOHN KNOX STATUE

towards modern computer science. He also drew up plans for a tank, an armoured car, a submarine and a kind of death ray which used lenses to concentrate the sun's heat on the enemy.

His polymath ingenuity was used in more domestic episodes. He discovered that poultry were being stolen from his Merchiston estate and suspected his servants. Using his reputation as a man of magic, he told them he was going to discover the true thief by locking the suspects in a room with his magic black cockerel. Every man had to stroke the bird, he ordered, and at the thief's touch it would crow loudly.

In the darkened room, the black cockerel made the rounds and Napier waited. When light was restored, he examined the hands of all present and found only one man's hands without the soot he had smeared on the cockerel's feathers and the thief was unmasked.

The 15th-century tower in which Napier lived and worked is now the centrepiece of the college of advanced education named after him in Colinton Road. Napier College was opened in 1964, exactly 350 years after the publication of *Mirifici Logarithmorum Canonis Descriptio*—a fitting tribute to the man and his work.

FAME IN THE WORLD OF FINANCE

Just 13 years younger than Napier was 'Jinglin' Geordie', George Heriot the goldsmith who became jeweller to James VI of Scotland and I of England and his consort, Anne of Denmark. Heriot is the most illustrious member of the Incorporation of Goldsmiths of the City of Edinburgh, which celebrated the tercentenary of its Royal Charter in 1987 and is the only guild in Scotland to have its own hallmark.

Jinglin' Geordie combined being the royal jeweller with the post of banker and moneylender to the royal family. When he died in London in 1623, he was a very rich man and his will made provisions for founding a children's home for the education and upbringing of orphans and fatherless children which has become George Heriot's School, built between 1628 and 1660, the finest Renaissance-style building in Edinburgh. There is also a pub named after him in Fleshmarket Close.

About this time the capital was gaining a reputation for influential bankers. William Paterson from Dumfriesshire was one of them. He founded the Bank of England in 1690 and was the prime mover in the disastrous Darien Scheme of 1698.

Before the Union of Parliaments in 1707, although they shared the same king, Scots were treated by the English as foreigners and debarred from trading with English colonies. In 1695, Paterson set up the Company of Scotland trading to Africa and the Indies as a proposed joint Scots and English company in London. The East India Company and other English traders vehemently opposed it and impeached its English founders for treachery. Scotland and its Parliament were furious and Paterson persuaded half Scotland to invest in a new project which would be for Scots alone, the Darien Scheme, a Scots colony in the Isthmus of Panama.

Unfortunately, the site was ill-chosen, its sovereignty challenged by Spain. The expedition which set out from

'HIGH' STREET

In the 18th century there was a fish and poultry market at the lower end of Old Fishmarket Close, which was described as a 'stinking ravine'. The town hangman once lived there, as did wealthy George Heriot (the founder of Heriot's hospital) and Daniel Defoe, author of *Robinson Crusoe*, who acted as a secret agent for the English government at the time of the Union of Parliaments.

GEORGE HERIOT

FAMOUS RESIDENTS

INSTANT SOUP

Street traders hawked their wares all over Edinburgh. One of their cries was: 'Twa dips and a wallop for a bawbee', which brought out the womenfolk with pails of boiling water into which a leg of mutton was dunked.

Leith in 1698 to establish it was inexperienced and unhelped by the indifference, where it was not hostility, of the English colonists in America and the Caribbean. Two thousand lives and all the money and goods invested in its creation were lost and the project abandoned in 1700.

Paterson himself survived the Darien expedition and returned to Scotland to become an advocate of union with England, a move which he had done as much as anyone to achieve by bankrupting half his countrymen.

John Law, born in 1671, was another financial wizard, with a talent for tennis and gambling. After a series of adventures which included killing a man in a duel in London, being imprisoned and sentenced to death, travelling extensively on the Continent, and making money speculating in securities and foreign exchange in Italy, Holland and Switzerland, he returned to Edinburgh and settled in his family home, Lauriston Castle.

He tried to persuade the Scottish Parliament to improve the stricken economy by issuing bank-notes but his suggestions were turned down and he set off again on his travels, to Brussels, Paris and his old haunt, Genoa, wheeling and dealing and writing works on political economy.

He offered his system for paying off the French National Debt to Louis XIV who rejected it on the somewhat illogical grounds that Law was not a Catholic.

A fervent advocate of bank-notes, he insisted that the secret of wealth for nations was 'to make gold out of paper' and in 1716 he set up a joint-stock bank with the connivance of the French Government and became a naturalised Frenchman. With the Company of the West he regulated and managed French trade with Louisiana and was responsible for founding the city of New Orleans. Honours were showered upon him. He was elected a member of the French Academy and is claimed to have been the first millionaire.

Adopting Henry of Navarre's dictum that 'Paris is worth a mass' he became a Roman Catholic and was appointed Controller-General of Finance to Louis XV and, although he was exiled after devaluation, he retired, apparently not too impoverished, to Venice where he died in 1729.

His family home, Lauriston Castle in Cramond Road South, is now owned by Edinburgh City and District Council.

ROBERT SIBBALD AND ANDREW BALFOUR

Edinburgh's Royal Botanic Gardens, among the finest in Europe, owe their creation to two 17th-century doctors, Robert Sibbald and Andrew Balfour, who planted medicinal herbs and plants in a Physic Garden near the Trinity Hospital in 1667. Over the years the garden was enlarged and extended in various locations in the New Town and moved to its present site in Inverleith in 1820.

A MUSICAL LEGACY

One of the few things to be said in favour of James VII and II is that while in Edinburgh as Duke of York and the King's Commissioner, in 1682 he instigated the first musical concerts in the tennis courts at Holyroodhouse.

SIR ROBERT SIBBALD

FAMOUS RESIDENTS

St Cecilia's Hall, in the Cowgate, which is still used for concerts and recitals today was opened in 1762. As well as being used during the Edinburgh Festival and at other times, it houses the Russell Collection of keyboard instruments, including harpsichords, clavichords, chamber organs, spinets, virginals and fortepianos belonging to the Faculty of Music at Edinburgh University.

'Fiddler Tam', Thomas Erskine, the 6th Earl of Kellie, was one of the prominent figures in Edinburgh's musical life of the time. A cheerful and boisterous character, renowned for his atrocious puns, he studied composition and the violin at Mannheim and wrote minuets for Edinburgh ladies which were popular south of the Border and on the Continent as well as in Scotland.

Another jolly figure, General John Reid, a Perthshire soldier who was a good flute player, left £52,000 in his will in 1807 to found a School of Music, still commemorated in the Reid Hall in the University. In 1841 the University made overtures to Felix Mendelssohn, who visited the city in 1829, to be the Reid Professor of Music, but Mendelssohn, busy in Leipzig and Berlin, politely declined.

SCOTLAND'S UNCROWNED KINGS

The 'men of genius' to be met in the High Street in the 18th century could have been painters, philosophers, writers, doctors, economists, engineers, sociologists, architects, geologists, lawyers, ministers or explorers.

They might have included two men, each known in his time as 'the uncrowned king of Scotland', Duncan Forbes of Culloden, and Henry Dundas, 1st Viscount Melville.

As Lord President of the Court of Session, Forbes strove for justice tempered with mercy after the Jacobite rebellion of 1745 against the kind of Hanoverian mentality exemplified by the Duke of Cumberland who called him 'that old woman who talked to me about humanity'. There is a superb statue by Roubiliac of Forbes laying down the law, beneath the hammer-beam roof of Parliament Hall in the High Street.

Henry Dundas stands on a pillar in the centre of St Andrew Square. He held several government offices under North and Pitt between 1777 and 1801 and survived impeachment in the House of Lords for his handling of the finances of the Navy.

He was widely known as Harry the Ninth. When Dundas was Home Secretary, that celebrated judge and diarist, Lord Cockburn said 'Henry Dundas, an Edinburgh man, and well calculated by talent and manner to make despotism popular, was the absolute dictator of Scotland and had the means of rewarding submission, and of supressing opposition, beyond what were ever exercised in modern times by one person, in any portion of the empire'.

THE COCKBURN ASSOCIATION

Henry Cockburn himself successfully defended the common-law wife of the bodysnatcher, Burke, and helped draft the Scottish Reform Bill. He loved life, good company and Edinburgh, and had a shrewd assessing eye for his fellow creatures, brilliantly demonstrated in his

SHOW HOUSE

History comes to life at the Edinburgh Wax Museum in the High Street. There are more than 150 figures, including many famous characters from Scottish history, from the 11th century to the present day. The collection is in a beautiful Georgian (1766) house frequented by Sir Walter Scott who attended lodge meetings there. In 1780 the building became the King's Arms Tavern and remained so for 12 years.

STATUE OF HENRY DUNDAS

contributions to the *Edinburgh Review* and in *Memorials of His Time*.

The novelist Evelyn Waugh and the journalist Claud Cockburn are among his descendants and The Cockburn Association, concerned with the preservation and conservation of the best in Edinburgh, commemorates its namesake's preoccupation with this cause, which among other things, saved the south side of Princes Street from being built upon.

POETS, THINKERS AND PIONEERS
There were poets galore — Robert Fergusson, whom Burns admired so much that he paid for his tombstone in Canongate Kirkyard; James Thomson who wrote *Rule Britannia*; Burns himself who was lionised in Edinburgh in 1786 and 1787; James Macpherson, the 'creator' of Ossian 'which ran like a flow of lava through Europe' according to Matthew Arnold. Macpherson was also praised by Schiller, Goethe, Ingres, Georges Sand, Mendelssohn and Brahms and adopted by Napoleon as his favourite poet.

Allan Ramsay the wigmaker, bookseller, playwright and poet lived here, as did his son of the same name, a distinguished portrait painter. Other local artists included Henry Raeburn and Alexander Nasmyth, famous as 'the father of Scottish landscape'.

Architects like Robert Adam and his family played their part in changing the appearance of the city. Charlotte Square, Register House and the entrance to the University are the most important Adam buildings. Thomas Telford worked on the New Town as a stone mason and studied the making of roads and bridges.

David Hume, the genial empiricist was keeper of the Advocates' Library and entertained Rousseau, Dr Johnson and Benjamin Franklin. Hume's friend, Adam Smith, invented political economy with *The Wealth of Nations* in 1776.

Several famous explorers have associations with Edinburgh. James Bruce 'The Abyssinian', who discovered the source of the Blue Nile studied law at the University in the 1740s and Mungo Park, explorer of the Niger, read medicine in 1789. Alexander Gordon Laing, the first European to reach Timbuctoo was also an Edinburgh student.

The 19th century brought photography and two of its pioneers, David Octavius Hill and Robert Thomson, lived and worked in Edinburgh.

LITERARY GIANTS — SCOTT AND STEVENSON
Sir Walter Scott, although born in the 18th century (1771), became known as an author only in the 19th when he published a series of romantic epic poems under his own name and later wrote historical novels under the pseudonum 'Waverley'.

Scott's first original work, the *Minstrelsy of the Scottish Border*, was published in 1803, when he was 31. In addition to the later 'Waverley Novels', as they were known, Scott wrote 11 more prose works—seven fictional and four historical. He also made translations from German, kept a journal and wrote numerous letters.

His novels had a profound influence all over the

ROBERT ADAM

literate world and created an interest in Scotland which surpassed even Ossian. Scott's novels rival Shakespeare as source material for opera.

The other major Edinburgh literary figure is Robert Louis Stevenson, son of a family of lighthouse builders. He intended to become a civil engineer but his health was not good enough to cope with the work. Instead he began studying at Edinburgh University.

Much less of a sentimentalist than Scott, he was a more astringent writer as he proved in his macabre, schizophrenic novel, *The Strange Case of Dr Jekyll and Mr Hyde* (based on an Edinburgh character, Deacon Brodie, who was a respectable town councillor by day and a burglar by night), in his essays and in *The New Arabian Nights*. That he could also write gripping adventure yarns, he showed with *Treasure Island* and *Kidnapped*.

SIR WALTER SCOTT

MEDICINE AND MORE

Although Edinburgh had established a reputation as a medical centre earlier, it was in the 19th century that it really came to the fore.

James Lind had shown the way with his *Treatise on the Scurvy* in 1753 with which he demonstrated how scurvy could be prevented by the juice of citrus fruits. James Gregory, one of a brilliant scientific family, invented Gregory's Mixture, a universal pharmaceutical comforter used up to recent times.

James Syme, Edinburgh's Professor of Clinical Surgery, the greatest surgeon of his day, was known as 'the Napoleon of Surgery'.

James Young Simpson discovered the use of chloroform as an anaesthetic, was the first to use it in childbirth and founded modern practice in gynaecology.

James Lister was Syme's assistant and married his daughter. Eventually he succeeded Syme as Professor of Surgery. His work on antiseptics earned him a baronetcy and later he was the first doctor to be made a peer.

James Miranda Stuart Barry began studying medicine in Edinburgh at the age of ten, disguised as a boy. She served 46 years in the armed services before, as a result of having yellow fever, she was discovered to be a woman. Her secret was kept by the doctor who examined her and she rose to become Inspector-General of Military Hospitals in Canada.

Sir Arthur Conan Doyle was from an Edinburgh family, studied medicine in the city and served as a field surgeon in the Boer War. But his celebrity came from his Sherlock Holmes stories, the central character of which was based on the investigative capacities of Edinburgh surgeon, Dr Joseph Bell.

However, Edinburgh characters do not end with Conan Doyle and famous visitors to the city are more numerous than ever.

Among well-known names to whom Edinburgh was their first home are actors Sean Connery, Alistair Sim and Ronnie Corbett; broadcasters Magnus Magnusson, Ludovic Kennedy and Tom Fleming, and composers Thea Musgrave and John Macleod.

There are many other names and you will not spend long in Scotland's capital before you have a few characters of your own to add to the historical list.

PLACES TO VISIT

Pocket Guide to EDINBURGH

PLACES TO VISIT • PLACES TO VISIT • PLACES TO VISIT • PLACES TO VISIT • PLACES TO VISIT • PLACES TO VISIT • PLACES TO VISIT •

46 BRIDGES IN EDINBURGH – CANONGATE TOLBOOTH

SOUTH BRIDGE

Bridges in Edinburgh

An early concern of 18th-century Edinburgh planners was how to cross the wide valley (now occupied by Waverley Station) and join Old and New Town. The foundation stone of the first North Bridge was laid in 1763, though because of a partial collapse through faulty foundations, the project was not completed until 1772. Today's bridge is a reconstruction of 1897. The continuation of this main route south, known to generations as 'The Bridges', was carried by South Bridge, only really conspicuous as a bridge from the Cowgate below. It is a 19-arch construction dating from 1788.

The continuation of a roadway south from the Mound was by means of George IV Bridge, completed in 1836 and involving the wholesale destruction of a number of historic closes in the Royal Mile.

Camera Obscura and Outlook Tower

Castle Hill

The lower storeys of this conspicuous building in Castlehill are 17th-century, while the upper floors with their 'castellations' were added around 1853 when an optician, Maria Theresa Short, devised and built a camera obscura. With modifications over the years, this device still operates today, giving a panoramic view over the city.

In the 1890s, the property was acquired and the facilities expanded by Sir Patrick Geddes, the Edinburgh-born architect and town-planning pioneer. Today, the Outlook Tower is a visitor centre with exhibitions and displays as well as its still popular camera obscura.

Canongate Church

Canongate

The Canongate Church dates from 1688 and is evidence of the formerly independent life of the burgh of Canongate. It was originally built for the congregation of the Abbey Church of Holyrood. The worshippers there were displaced when the Catholic King James VII of Scotland (II of England) ordered its conversion to a chapel for the Knights of the Thistle. Between 1946 and 1953 Canongate Church was extensively restored and the Market Cross of the burgh was rebuilt in the churchyard. The poet, Robert Fergusson, the economist, Adam Smith and Robert Burns' 'Clarinda' are among notable Scots buried there.

Canongate Tolbooth

Canongate

The Canongate Tolbooth was the civic centre of the burgh of Canongate, which had an independent status outside Edinburgh's town walls. Though there is evidence of a Tolbooth earlier than the late 15th century, the one surviving today was rebuilt in 1591 to include a Council Chamber. This was on the first floor, reached by the outside stairs. In 1840, a few years before the burgh merged with the city of Edinburgh, the Canongate Tolbooth's use as a council meeting place was discontinued. Between 1842 and 1848 it was an overflow for the Calton Jail, before undergoing restoration in 1879. It is now another of the city's museums, with the planned exhibitions and displays on the history of trade unions and local history due for completion in 1988.

Charlotte Square

Widely held to be one of Europe's finest examples of civic architecture, Charlotte Square was planned in 1791 by Robert Adam, a year before his death. His brother, James, died in 1794 and, as a result, the original plan for symmetrical façades on the north and south sides was not rigidly followed.

The palace-fronted north side, which commands attention as the finest part of the square, was built fairly closely to the original plan. On this north side are the official residence of the Secretary of State for Scotland, the headquarters of the National Trust for Scotland and the Trust's Georgian House.

Churches in Edinburgh

Of Edinburgh's many churches, those listed below are near the city centre. Others listed separately in this gazetteer include St Giles and Tron Churches.

St Andrew's & St George's Church, George Street Of interest not only because of its fine design, but because its site in George Street was a second choice.

Originally, it was intended for the east side of St Andrew Square, balancing St George's (now West Register House) on the west side of Charlotte Square—and in keeping with the overall symmetry of Craig's New Town plan. However, a wealthy and influential baronet, Sir Lawrence Dundas, procured, by dubious means, the site for his own mansion. This still stands as the headquarters of the Royal Bank of Scotland, while St Andrew's was relegated to nearby George Street.

St Cuthbert's Church, Lothian Road Built on the ancient site of the Culdee Church of St Cuthbert dating from the 8th century, this religious building has seen much rebuilding. It was damaged during a siege of the Castle in 1689, rebuilt in 1775 and again in 1892. Almost all of Edinburgh was in its parish till 1834. Its graveyard has an interesting watchtower. Nearby is St John's Church, a Gothic Revival building of 1816.

St Mary's Cathedral, Palmerston Place A comparatively late arrival to the Edinburgh skyline, St Mary's Cathedral is impressively seen along the length of Melville Street near the West End. Its foundations were laid in 1874 and its

ST MARY'S CATHEDRAL

spires only added in 1917. It is said to be the largest ecclesiastical building constructed in Scotland since the Reformation.

St Stephen's Church, St Vincent Street Prominent at the foot of Howe Street and conspicuous from Frederick Street above, this large church is said to have been built in 1826 by the city authorities deliberately to block the view of the handsome façade of Edinburgh Academy, immediately behind it and erected three years before.

This uncharitable gesture by the authorities apparently resulted from the Edinburgh Academy's opening as a privately funded rival to the Town Council's own Royal High School!

City Art Centre

Market Street

A handsome former warehouse, originally intended to store newsprint for The Scotsman newspaper next door, is now the home of Edinburgh's own fine art collection.

This collection comprises about 3,000 paintings, drawings, prints and sculptures, mostly by Scottish artists, from the 17th century to the present. Views of Edinburgh, portraits of its famous citizens and numerous other items of historical significance are also well represented and there is a wide-ranging exhibition programme.

Opposite the Art Centre is the Fruitmarket Gallery, likewise in a converted warehouse, which also offers a widely varied programme, concentrating mainly on contemporary Scottish and international fine art. It is well worth a visit.

Calton Hill

At just over 350ft (110m) Edinburgh's Calton Hill is hardly a dominating height, yet it stands conspicuously on a sight-line along Princes Street and commands attention by the extraordinary architecture scattered across its domed top. It also looks particularly striking from Salisbury Crags in Holyrood Park, when the impressive façade of the former Royal High School, strung along the base of the hill, echoes the columns of the monuments on top. Equally eye-catching is the completely different aspect from Ferry Road to the north near Goldenacre, with Arthur's Seat itself providing an imposing background.

It is probably the best place for a city view with the minimum of effort. Visitors can walk up a steep, stepped path from Waterloo Place, the continuation of Princes Street, or drive up a curving road which starts just before the former Royal High School. The hill was said to be one of the favourite viewpoints of Robert Louis Stevenson, a writer who knew the area well. (His cousins lived in nearby Royal Terrace and, as a child, Stevenson often played in the adjacent gardens.)

In Stevenson's time, the hill would have presented much the same appearance as it does today. Its extravagant collection dates mainly from the latter half of the 18th century and into the first decades of the 19th century, when a great enthusiasm for neo-classicism gripped the city and its architects. The columns and temples of Calton Hill certainly helped Edinburgh earn its reputation as 'the Athens of the north'.

The strange unfinished grandeur of the National Monument is the hill's most conspicuous feature. Designed by Playfair, it was intended to be a model of the Parthenon on the Acropolis in Athens and a monument to the dead of the Napoleonic Wars. The foundation stone was laid in 1822, but by 1830 money had run out. The 12 pillars of locally quarried stone now stand as a monument to high hopes but unsuccessful fund-raising. Though they have earned such titles as 'Edinburgh's Disgrace' and 'Scotland's Pride and Poverty' they contribute greatly to the drama of the city skyline.

The earliest building on the hill is the Old Observatory of 1766. This was designed by James Craig, the designer of the competition-winning street layout of the original New Town. By contrast, Craig's Old Observatory forsakes neo-classical preoccupations and is instead in a Gothic style, with little castellations. Before astronomical observations were moved to Blackford Hill, a New Observatory was built, this time designed by the prolific Playfair in 1818. It is easily identified as the conspicuous cross-shaped temple. Visitors encounter the architect again in the less imposing Playfair Monument, noted as part of the Observatory perimeter wall. This was to the architect's uncle, John Playfair, mathematician and natural philosopher, who was influential in the building of the Observatory in the first place.

The visitor has yet more Playfair to note. He designed the circular little hilltop temple in 1830 as a monument to Dugald Stewart, one-time Professor of Moral Philosophy. It was inspired by the Lysicrates Monument from 4th-century Athens—clearly a very inspiring piece, as it was also used as a model for the monument to Robert Burns on Regent Road below, this time by Thomas Hamilton in 1830.

One more conspicuous monument catches the visitor's eye. This is the Nelson Monument, its upturned telescope shape entirely appropriate and designed by Robert Burn (not to be confused with the poet, but the father of the better-known architect, William). Built in 1816, the Nelson Monument has a time-ball on top—a device which, after being hoisted up by machinery, drops on the stroke of one o'clock. It is said to have been originally intended as a time-check for sailors in the port of Leith.

Calton Hill offers almost a complete panorama, with only the bulk of Arthur's Seat interrupting the views to distant horizons. The Lomond Hills of Fife are visible across the Forth in one direction, while in the other, the Pentlands can be seen beyond the spire of St Giles. To the east, along the crescent shape of the East Lothian coastline, the Berwick Law and the Bass Rock are visible. Like Arthur's Seat and the Calton Hill itself, they are volcanic in origin.

Among the nearer landmarks close by the hill is the Old Calton Burial Ground, divided in two in 1815 by the opening of Waterloo Place, with the Regent Bridge joining Princes Street to the flanks of the Calton Hill. The prominent obelisk is the Martyrs' Monument, designed by Thomas Hamilton in 1844 to commemorate political martyrs of 1793. Also in the Old

Burial Ground are a number of other monuments, including one to David Hume, the philosopher, by Robert Adam (1777).

The comparatively modern St Andrew's House (1937), on the southern flanks of the hill, east of the Old Burial Ground, was built on the site of the Calton Jail. The Governor's House with its comic battlements has survived and perches above the steep slopes overlooking Waverley Station.

The trees immediately to the east are in the gardens of Royal Terrace, which along with Calton Terrace and Regent Terrace make up a late phase of New Town building. The north-facing Royal Terrace is the longest continuous neo-classical frontage to be found anywhere in Edinburgh. It was intended to overlook a further stately development running down to the sea at Leith—though as the visitor will readily note from the Calton Hill vantage point, this other grand New Town was never built.

City Chambers

Royal Mile

The City Chambers were completed in 1761 and were thus a very early development in the great wave of new building which resulted in Edinburgh's New Town to the north. Though the frontage as seen from the High Street is impressive, the rear of the building rises a spectacular 12 storeys from Cockburn Street. In the Piazza is a statue of Alexander with his horse, Bucephalus.

The building was originally conceived as the Royal Exchange—a place where merchants, lawyers and other branches of commerce could meet for business. During its construction, excavated material was taken up the Royal Mile and used as foundations for the Castle Esplanade. However, as a commercial venue the Royal Exchange was not successful and was taken over by the Town Council in 1811. Shops lingered on in the forecourt and in the arches until the end of the century.

Colinton

A former milling village, Colinton bridges the gap between town and country with its wooded walkway along the banks of the Water of Leith. Particularly picturesque in autumn, the path partly utilises the now-vanished railway branch line which, when it opened, helped make this village 'desirable' to wealthy commuters.

The local parish church of 1771 was once the ministry of the Reverend Dr Lewis Balfour, maternal grandfather of the writer, Robert Louis Stevenson, and often visited by him as a boy. The author recalls in an essay many details of the church and manse which can still be seen today.

Corstorphine

Now a suburb of the city, the former village of Corstorphine was once separated from it by a loch and marsh to the west of the Water of Leith. Travellers were guided across the marshes by a lamp in the tower of Corstorphine Church (now a symbolic electric lamp). No trace remains of Corstorphine Castle except for some fine old trees and a well-preserved doo'cot (dovecote) on the former estate. As well as the old village's farming interests it once had a sulphurous spring which gained it minor prominence as a spa resort. It had lost both its spring and its loch by the 1830s. Corstorphine is also the home of the Edinburgh Tapestry Company, founded by the son of William Morris in 1910.

Craigmillar Castle

Though more than a little overshadowed by Edinburgh Castle, and in less attractive surroundings from the visitor's viewpoint, Craigmillar Castle (AM) is, nevertheless, a fine example of a fortified baronial house. It is also of considerable historic significance. Mary, Queen of Scots retreated here after the murder of Rizzio. The plot for the murder of her second husband, Darnley, was also hatched here. Mary herself came here from Jedburgh in 1566 and there is a room known as Queen Mary's chamber.

Among several other incidents, the castle itself was captured and burned by the Earl of Hertford in 1544.

Originally in the hands of the Preston family, who built the central L-plan tower in 1374, the castle was strengthened in 1427 with curtain walls all around. Further defences were added after Hertford's raid and later rebuilding took place in the 17th century.

Cramond

Known as *Alaterva* to the Romans, Cramond, at the mouth of the little River Almond, was once a port used while the Antonine Wall was under construction further up the Forth. Later developments all but destroyed a Roman fort here, though a variety of Roman artefacts have been uncovered nearby. Further upstream is evidence of its later industrial role as a once-thriving ironworks, with water-powered mills. Still visible are the remains of the small docks into which vessels took coal and ores and left with steel and wrought iron. This activity was at a peak in the 18th century. The remains of some of the mills can be seen in the pleasant leafy walk upstream. Today, visitors come to enjoy the views across the Firth of Forth, the pleasant environs of the neat, white-washed cottages and to admire the yachts of the local club.

Dean Village

One of Edinburgh's surprises is the environs of this former milling community on the banks of the Water of Leith only a few minutes' walk from Princes Street. No mills now operate, but the work of the Baxters (bakers) with their trade guild is recalled in several existing features such as their badge cut in the stonework of the narrow bridge over the Water of Leith.

This bridge and the steep road down, Bell's Brae, were formerly the main route out of Edinburgh to the north until the building of the Dean Bridge by Telford (1832) which still carries today's traffic. Though overshadowed and bypassed, the little village should not be overlooked. Visitors can join the Water of Leith walkway here. Downstream, the pathway leaves the village, passes under the Dean Bridge, goes past St Bernard's Well and emerges at Stockbridge.

Duddingston

Tucked beyond the bulk of Arthur's Seat, the once isolated village of Duddingston, formerly a weaving community, reveals its antiquity in a number of interesting features. The most conspicuous of these is its church, Norman in origin. Though greatly altered, its richly carved doorway remains. Its churchyard still has a watchtower to guard against bodysnatchers, while at the gate of the church a pair of 'jougs' survive. These consist of an iron collar, attached to the wall by a chain. Wrongdoers were clamped into it in full view. Also close by is a 'loupin' on stane' or mounting block.

The ancient Sheep's Heid Inn is found in the village and claims the oldest skittle alley in Scotland. Nearby is Duddingston Loch, a bird sanctuary since 1923, now in the care of the Scottish Wildlife Trust.

Edinburgh Castle

The shape of the Castle Rock is the result of an eastward moving glacier scouring round the hard volcanic rock to form three steep sides and a long ramp pointing east. This formed the Royal Mile. The process is called a 'crag and tail' by geologists. The crag became the Castle Rock, while the tail slopes down to Holyrood. Inevitably, with such strong defensive possibilities, the site has been occupied since the very earliest times, probably originally by Iron Age peoples.

The Romans, however, seemed to have built their main fortifications elsewhere. Picts and Saxons in an early power-struggle may each have occupied the site, but by the 7th century Edwin of Northumbria had built a castle. In the 10th century the Castle Rock was part of the kingdom of Alba and became thoroughly Scottish after King Malcolm defeated the Northumbrians in 1018. Thereafter, facts become more easily separated from early legend. Malcolm's wife, the saintly Queen Margaret, died in the Castle in 1093. She had been instrumental in persuading King Malcolm to move the royal court from Dunfermline to Edinburgh.

Her chapel still survives on the highest point of the Castle Rock and, though greatly rebuilt, remains as one of Scotland's oldest ecclesiastical buildings. Little else has survived from those early days. The tumult of wars and sieges right down to the Jacobite rebellions in the 18th century have inevitably wrought great changes in the appearance of the Castle.

For example, its Esplanade, the grand setting of the spectacular Military Tattoo, was built in 1753 with material excavated during the building of the Royal Exchange. Before that, the approach to the Castle had been much steeper. Similarly, the Gatehouse is a Victorian addition, with the statues of Robert the Bruce and William Wallace, two of Scotland's

EDINBURGH CASTLE

greatest heroes, placed on guard there only in 1929, during the celebrations to mark the city's 600th anniversary as a Royal Burgh. The Portcullis Gate beyond is on the site of the Constable's Tower, destroyed during 1573 when Kirkcaldy of Grange held the Castle for Mary, Queen of Scots.

This particularly destructive incident also resulted in the building of the conspicuous Half-Moon Battery, erected just after the successful siege by the Regent Morton. Again, it was built on a fortification destroyed by cannon—David's Tower of 1367, which had withstood the forces of the English Kings Richard II in 1385 and Henry IV in 1400. The firepower of the Half-Moon Battery overlooks the houses of the Old Town and was understandably unpopular with the early citizens.

The Castle's last siege was during the 1745 Rebellion. While Bonnie Prince Charlie enjoyed himself in the Palace of Holyrood House, at the other end of the Royal Mile the Castle's garrison held out for the Hanoverian government. At the end of October, an unknown soldier must have fired the last shot in anger as the Prince and his forces rode out of town—and the Castle's strategic role in military conflict came to an end.

The Castle still has a substantial military presence, including the headquarters of the Royal Scots and the Royal Scots Dragoon Guards. Some of the buildings, including office and mess accommodation, are not open to public inspection. Visitors can trace much military history in the nearby United Services Museum, founded in 1933, which contains many relics. Also notable is the Scottish National War Memorial, designed by Sir Robert Lorimer and opened in 1927. It is built on the site of the Castle's own church. There are plenty of other places of interest for the visitor to see on the Castle Rock, including the Great Hall, built by James IV in the early 16th century, though somewhat over-restored since. It housed the Scottish Parliament before Parliament House was built. The need to find a level space for the Great Hall resulted in great vaults being built beneath. They have become known as the French Prisons as they held French prisoners of war during the Napoleonic Wars. Graffiti written by their French occupants can still be seen.

Also below ground and protected from the weather is the famous Mons Meg, now in the vaults. This 15th-century cannon has a variety of explanations of its origins, but what is known is that it burst during the firing of a salute to the Duke of York in 1682 and lay derelict before it was taken to the Tower of London in 1754. Through the influence of Sir Walter Scott it was returned to the Castle in 1829.

Sir Walter was responsible for the recovery of even more important Scottish artefacts. The Scottish crown, sceptre and sword of state, the Regalia of Scotland, were locked away in a trunk in 1707 at the Union of the Crowns. They lay dusty and forgotten until Scott obtained permission from the King in distant London to search for them. Now they are on display in the Crown Room, which is part of the Palace and King's Lodging on one side of the Crown Square. The name of this building is a reminder that it was once the royal residence in Edinburgh.

One of the most obvious customs connected with the Castle may cause momentary alarm to casual visitors strolling in Princes Street or its gardens. The firing of the One o' Clock Gun on weekdays dates back to 1848 and its unexpectedly loud report echoes round the streets of the New Town. Since 1861 it has been connected electrically to the fall of a time-ball seen on top of the Nelson Monument on Calton Hill—just one of the city's landmarks which can be seen from the Castle ramparts. With the unmistakable outline of the Castle adding so much to Edinburgh's unique skyline—particularly when floodlit on a summer evening—it is hardly surprising that this high vantage point offers superb views, as far as hills such as Ben Ledi and Ben Vorlich beyond the Highland line.

EDINBURGH ZOO

Edinburgh Zoo

On the south-facing slopes of Corstorphine Hill is the Royal Zoological Society of Scotland's Edinburgh Zoo, covering 70 acres. It was founded in 1913. Its most famous exhibit is its colony of both king and gentoo penguins, which take their famous walk, the 'Penguin Parade', round part of the zoo every day during the summer months.

George Heriot's School

George Heriot had a tiny workshop along the north side of St Giles, in the line of booths known as the krames, which survived until 1817. More importantly, he was also goldsmith to King James VI. Through his gold and jewellery trade, 'Jinglin' Geordie' amassed a fortune and arranged through a trust that it was used to create a 'hospital for the maintenance, relief, bringing-up and educating poor fatherless boys . . .'

Heriot died in 1623; his hospital/school was duly built by 1650, promptly occupied by Cromwell's sick and injured troops for the next eight years, then received its first pupils in the following year. The Heriot Trust went on to open other schools and George Heriot's Hospital was renamed George Heriot's School in 1886. It remains today, south of the Grassmarket, and its distinctive turrets can be seen from the Castle.

The Georgian House

Charlotte Square

Part of the magnificent façade on the north side of Charlotte Square, No. 7 has been restored by the National Trust for Scotland. It re-creates, down to the finest detail, a Georgian town house of around 1800, that is, when the building was new and in the very height of fashion. Furniture, fabrics and décor are correct for the period and provide a fascinating insight into the customs and lifestyle of the times, not only in the elegant public rooms, but in the labour-intensive kitchen below stairs.

Gladstone's Land

Castle Hill

This six-storey tenement on the Lawnmarket preserves its original arcaded front of around 1631—a unique survival of a feature once common in Scottish domestic architecture. It was built by a merchant, Thomas Gledstanes, who rebuilt an even earlier structure, traces of which are still visible inside the building today.

Today's visitors can also see unusual original ceiling and wall paintings and original fireplaces. The building was acquired by the National Trust for Scotland in 1934 and is now renovated and refurbished as a typical house of a 17th-century merchant.

Grassmarket

King James III of Scotland granted a charter to hold markets in the Grassmarket in 1477. Though just south of the castle, at that time the area still lay outside the town walls. Later it was contained by the Flodden Wall of 1514–1560. The main road from the west ran through the Grassmarket, entering by the West Port, a name which survives today. Though a place of commerce through the centuries, it was also the scene of many hangings. The gallows' site is marked today by railings and a rose-coloured cross set into the cobble-stones. Among the surviving buildings is the White Hart Inn, where Robert Burns and, later, William Wordsworth stayed on their visits to the city.

Originally, to reach the Castle via the Lawnmarket, the traveller had to go up the West Bow, which twisted steeply up from the east end of the Grassmarket, but the Victorian development of Victoria Street cut through this old thoroughfare. Now the Grassmarket end of the West Bow leads into Victoria Street, while the top end, the Upper Bow, can still be found leading off the Lawnmarket, connected to the lower level by a flight of steps. Victoria Street itself is an interesting shopping street, with a fine variety of craft, antique, print and other unusual shops.

Greyfriars Bobby

Greyfriars Bobby was a Skye terrier who was devoted to his master, a local police constable, John Gray. After his master's death in 1858, the dog lingered near his grave in Greyfriars Churchyard for 14 years. In doing so he became a local celebrity, going daily to be fed at a nearby restaurant on hearing the one o'clock gun! (This was probably good for business.) So popular was the faithful Bobby that the Lord Provost himself paid for his licence. The dog so moved the citizens of Edinburgh that in 1873 a bronze statue, by William Brodie, was erected to the faithful animal. To this day it stands near the churchyard, on the junction of Candlemaker Row and George IV Bridge. Items associated with Bobby, including his collar and dish, are preserved in Huntly House Museum.

Greyfriars Church

Along with its churchyard, this church occupies the site of an earlier Franciscan monastery. It played an important part in Scottish religious history as the place where the National Covenant was signed in 1638, which plunged the nation soon after into drawn-out religious wars.

About 1,200 Covenanters, captured at the Battle of Bothwell Brig in 1679, were held here without shelter for five months, while other martyrs to the Covenanters' cause are commemorated in memorials within the walls. Greyfriars Church itself first opened for worship in 1620, was desecrated by Cromwell's troops in 1650, had a New Church built and attached to its west end in 1721, burned down in 1845 and was subsequently restored. Finally Old and New Churches were united in 1928.

Heart of Midlothian

High Street

Look for the cobbled stones set in a heart-shape on the High Street between St Giles and George IV Bridge. This marks the spot of the Old Tolbooth, latterly the town prison, demolished in 1817. The outline of the building is also marked on the road with brass plates. It is remembered as the Heart of Midlothian following the description of it in Sir Walter Scott's novel of the same name.

Hillend Ski Centre

Fairmilehead

Beyond the suburb of Fairmilehead on the north-facing slope of the Pentland Hills is the Hillend Ski Centre, with the longest artificial ski slope in Britain, dropping from around 1,200ft (370m) and popular throughout the year. Its chairlift offers non-skiers easy access to the Pentland Hills and magnificent views across the city and the Firth of Forth to Fife and beyond.

HOLYROOD PARK – JOHN KNOX HOUSE

Holyrood Park & Arthur's Seat

The rough slopes of Arthur's Seat would be a scenic asset in any part of Scotland. That they are a few minutes from Edinburgh's city centre is a bonus for visitors and residents alike. They provide an easy escape into the countryside, interest for the geologist and naturalist and fine views for everyone from many parts of this royal park. Formerly the King's or Queen's Park, it was first enclosed by King James V as a preserve for royal game.

Its highest point is the summit of Arthur's Seat, 822ft (253m) high. Its distinctive shape owes much to its volcanic origin about 235 million years ago. The summit, the so-called 'Lion's Head', along with the lower 'Lion's Haunch' were two volcanic vents, the more rounded Whinny Hill to the east was the volcanic cone with its stepped lava ridges. The formations were subsequently tilted by major earth movements and later molten rock pushed through the strata to form, after much erosion, the sill of Salisbury Crags.

A number of factors have resulted in its present appearance. These include generations of grazing, now closely controlled, the insensitive quarrying of Salisbury Crags—which a series of law-suits between 1819 and 1831 finally stopped—and the building of the Radical Road. Sir Walter Scott is credited with the original idea for this project—a roadway, built in 1820, which encircles the park at high level. The road recalls the radical views of the weavers and other tradesmen who were employed in this early 'job-creation' scheme. Both Dunsapie, high on the hill, and St Margaret's Lochs are artificial, created last century by damming and drainage. Visitors should note that there is also a one-way drive, which shortens the climb to the top of Arthur's Seat.

Though traces of early settlement have been found in the past, and the park was the site of several hilltop forts, the stones have long since been removed. Early cultivation terraces are noticeable on the east side of the hill, particularly when lit by a low sun. Much later are the remains of St Anthony's Chapel, overlooking St Margaret's Loch. It dates from around 1430 and fell into disuse at the time of the Reformation. Also of interest, on the north side of Salisbury Crags near Holyrood Palace, is St Margaret's Well, moved in 1862 from Restalrig, as it was in the way of developments on the North British Railway.

There are numerous walks for visitors in the park. The summit can be reached from the Queen's Drive, or from near St Anthony's Chapel. There is a footpath running high along the base of Salisbury Crags—and another route along the cliff tops. Visitors wandering on Whinny Hill can lose sight of the city entirely, as they can also in Hunter's Bog, at the foot of the long dip slope behind Salisbury Crags. Botanists will look out for such unusual plants as Red German Catchfly and Maiden Pink, while birdwatchers will enjoy a wide variety of species particularly around Duddingston Loch. Visitors interested in geology should note the protected sites in the old quarries on the crags, as well as Samson's Ribs—conspicuous dolerite columns on the cliff-face, seen clearly from the Queen's Drive on the way to Duddingston. Full details of the natural history of the park can be found in the Scottish Wildlife Trust's Visitor Centre, near the Palace gates.

Huntly House

Canongate

One of the best-preserved 16th-century buildings in the Old Town, Huntly House, overlooking the Canongate, was rebuilt in 1570 from earlier work. In the 18th century it became the headquarters of one of the city's guilds, the Hammermen (smiths) of the Canongate. In 1924 it was bought by the city and later became the most important museum of local history, with a wide-ranging collection including silver, glassware, pottery, shop signs and other trade artefacts as well as many relics from other demolished buildings.

Its name recalls an association with the first Marquess of Huntly, who is supposed to have lived there in the 16th century, though not all historians agree on this point.

John Knox House

High Street

This is a fine example of pre-Reformation domestic architecture dating from around the beginning of the 16th century. Some historians doubt that John Knox himself actually ever lived in it—though it is certainly old enough. Nevertheless, it

JOHN KNOX HOUSE – MALLENY GARDENS

JOHN KNOX HOUSE

was only a strongly-held belief that he died there in 1572 that preserved the building when it was about to be demolished in 1849.

Its projecting gallery at first-floor level is the only surviving example of what was once a common feature in Edinburgh's High Street. The initials inscribed on the outside are those of James Mossman (and his wife), goldsmith to Mary, Queen of Scots. Today, the house is a museum which includes painted panelling discovered in a recent restoration.

Lady Stair's House

Bank Street

This town house of 1622 is the only surviving building of the original Lady Stair's Close. At one stage in the late 18th century, the close became the main route connecting the nearby Lawnmarket—part of the Royal Mile—with the developing New Town via the Mound. Earlier, the house itself was owned by the widow of the first Earl of Stair, Lady Stair, who died in 1759.

The building was bought by Lord Rosebery in 1895 and presented to the city in 1907. It is currently a museum containing artefacts associated with the lives of three famous literary Scots: Robert Louis Stevenson, Sir Walter Scott and Robert Burns.

Lauriston Castle

Cramond Road South

This intriguing example of the Edwardian age is held in trust by the City of Edinburgh. The tower house of 1590, with its extensive Jacobean extension by William Burn in 1827, and later library, still retains the atmosphere of a gracious country mansion. The library is entered from the visitors' waiting room through a concealed door in a bookcase.

The peaceful grounds offer pleasant walks overlooking the Firth of Forth near Cramond and its extensive lawns are used by the Edinburgh Croquet Club.

Today's visitors can enjoy the conservative Edwardian interiors with their period furniture, Derbyshire Blue John ornaments, Crossley wool 'mosaics' and minor *objets d'art*.

Leith

The ancient seaport of the capital, Leith lost its independent status as recently as 1920—though it had only gained it in 1833. Incidents from its turbulent past include the arrival by sea of many famous figures in Scottish history, among them most of the Stuart monarchs—Mary, Queen of Scots arrived in 1561. The previous year the port had been besieged in battles between French Catholic troops under Mary's mother, Mary of Guise, and Protestant forces. It was occupied by Cromwell's troops in 1650. George IV disembarked at Leith in 1822.

The townsfolk once enjoyed golf on its still-surviving links and horse-racing on its sands. The Honourable Company of Edinburgh Golfers, one of the very first golf clubs, built premises in Leith in 1768. Nevertheless, the town has been predominantly a commercial port and, until recently, recession, decline of traditional local industries and insensitive redevelopment took their toll.

Now, a new consciousness of Leith's heritage has awakened and the area is becoming distinctly fashionable. Commercial, civic and domestic architecture has been extensively refurbished and Leith now offers the sort of nightlife in restaurants and bars that will match anything available anywhere near Princes Street.

Malleny Gardens

Balerno

In Balerno, on the outskirts of the city, the garden is laid out around a 17th-century house (not on view) built for Sir James Murray of Kilbaberton. It offers an interesting woodland walk and a good collection of shrub roses.

Meadowbank Sports Centre

Only a few minutes from the city centre, Edinburgh's major sports complex, originally built for the Commonwealth Games of 1970, includes a 15,000-seat stadium (8,000 covered). It offers a wide range of facilities and a temporary membership scheme for visitors.

The Meadows

This tree-studded parkland, now used for sports, funfairs, festivals and other recreation, was once a loch, the South or Borough Loch, finally drained in 1740. It was the scene of the first British international exhibition held outside London—the International Exhibition of Industry, Science and Art, staged in 1886. Two and a half million people visited the event, which had 7 acres of buildings, including a Grand Hall with seating for 10,000. Unfortunately the builders had not reckoned on an Act of Parliament which vetoed building on the Meadows—everything, including the hall, had to be demolished immediately the exhibition finished!

Today's visitors should look for the pillars at the western end of Melville Drive, erected by the local stonemasons' guild, the sundial commemorating the exhibition opening by Prince Albert and the whalebones on Jawbone Walk, presented by the Zetland Fair Isle Knitting Stand!

Adjacent, to the south, is Bruntsfield Links, more undulating parkland, and the site of one of the city's very earliest golf courses, dating from around 1695, though records go back a century earlier. The Bruntsfield Links Golfing Society dates from 1761. Since 1890 a short-hole pitch and putt course has been in existence here.

The Mound

An 18th-century Edinburgh tailor, George Boyd, was the first to see the need for an easy crossing between the Old Town, running down from the Castle, and the blossoming New Town to the north. Between them lay the muddy quagmire of the former Nor' Loch, then in the process of being drained—Princes Street Gardens and the railway occupy the site today.

Being anxious to give his New Town customers an easy passage to his Old Town shop, Boyd and some neighbours began making their own rough causeway. This project was taken up by the city authorities and orders were given for the construction of a huge ramp, made from the excavated material from the New Town building programme which was dumped on the site. When completed in 1830, it was estimated that the Mound contained over two million cartloads! First the Royal Scottish Academy, then the National Gallery were built to enhance the lower end of the Mound, while the top still gives a fine view over Princes Street. 'Geordie Boyd's Mud Brig' remains a vital link between the Old and the New.

Museum of Childhood

High Street

One of Edinburgh's most attractive museums, the unique Museum of Childhood in the High Street fascinates visitors of all ages. In 1986 it re-opened after major alteration and expansion which doubled its display area and now includes a restored Georgian Theatre. Toys, dolls, games and all the paraphernalia of childhood through the ages have made this museum internationally famous.

National Gallery of Scotland

The Mound

One of two fine neo-classical buildings by Playfair on the Mound, the National Gallery is one of Europe's finest smaller galleries with a distinguished collection of Old Masters, Impressionist and Scottish paintings. In addition to the two main viewing areas, there is a library and facilities for viewing works not on public display.

The architect William Playfair's earlier work, now the Royal Scottish Academy, is adjacent to the National Gallery, on the Princes Street end of the Mound, and mounts its own exhibition annually.

National Library of Scotland

George IV Bridge

Widely used by historians and other researchers, the National Library of Scotland is the fourth largest in Britain and has the privilege of receiving a copy of every work published in Britain. Its 'parent' was the Advocates' Library, founded in 1682 for the benefit of Scotland's legal profession. In 1925 the Advocates' Library transferred all its non-legal works to the nation, thus forming the National Library.

National Museums of Scotland

Royal Museum of Scotland, *Chambers Street* Formerly the Royal Scottish Museum, it shows the influence of London's Crystal Palace in its elegant, soaring, cast-iron columns and balconies. Within its airy, spacious interior, with many halls and galleries, is an extremely wide-ranging collection, including decorative arts of the world, archaeology, ethnography, natural history, geology, technology and science. There is also a programme of special exhibitions as well as gallery talks, lectures and films.

Royal Museum of Scotland, *Queen Street* Formerly the National Museum of Antiquities, this museum traces the story of Scotland from the Stone Age right up to modern times, by way of the earliest artefacts from prehistory, through the Picts, Romans and Vikings, and on to the Dark Ages and the Middle Ages. More recently recorded history on display includes relics of Mary, Queen of Scots and Bonnie Prince Charlie.

Sharing the same fine red sandstone building (1889) as the Royal Museum of Scotland (Queen Street), the **National Portrait Gallery** serves to bring to life many famous historical figures—the nation's kings and queens, rebels, Highland chiefs, political and literary figures, from the days of Queen Margaret right down to the 20th century—in a very wide-ranging collection. There is also an extensive reference facility with engravings and photographs of many portraits.

Palace of Holyroodhouse

Legend tells that the Scottish King David I was out hunting in the then darkly forested slopes of Holyrood Park when he was attacked and unhorsed by a wounded stag. Suddenly, a crucifix appeared between its antlers, the king grasped it and the stag fled. (This legend occurs in European literature attached to other places and saints.) In thanksgiving, the king founded the Abbey of Holyrood in 1128 and it adopted the stag and cross on its seal, as did the later burgh of Canongate nearby, which sprang up as a result of the Abbey.

King Edward of England burned the Abbey in 1322, and this fate at the hands of English invaders befell it again in 1544 and 1547. Just after Mary, Queen of Scots' association with it, the Scottish Reformers did as much damage by demolishing the choir and transepts, around 1569. In the 17th century King James VII converted it to a Roman Catholic Chapel Royal. It was violated again by a Presbyterian faction shortly after. As late as 1758 a new stone roof was built—but this collapsed only 10 years later. Today, 12th- or early 13th-century features include the north wall of the roofless nave and the great west doorway. The traceried windows are 17th-century.

The Palace of Holyroodhouse, which overlaps the outlines of the old religious buildings, grew originally from the Abbey guest house. It, too, has had a stormy history, bound up with the story of Scotland's Stuart monarchy. Holyroodhouse was founded by King James IV at the end of the 15th century, subsequently extended by his son, James V, damaged, like the Abbey, by the Earl of Hertford's raids in 1544 and 1547 but repaired for Mary, Queen of Scots, who held court here between 1561 and 1567.

After the Union of the Crowns with England in 1603, Holyrood no longer had a monarch in residence. In 1650, fire damaged the Palace while it was occupied by Cromwell's troops. Though Cromwell was responsible for some reconstruction, Charles II in 1671 ordered the rebuilding and redesigning which resulted in the façade seen today. Even then, it still saw some drama—an anti-

Catholic mob ran rampage in it in 1688 and Prince Charles Edward Stuart held court here in 1745—even though the Castle, at the other end of the Royal Mile, held out against him.

Though George IV stayed in 1822, the royal residence was then in decline, with the emphasis on other parts of the growing city. However, Queen Victoria and later King George V renewed interest, with subsequent redecoration and revitalisation of the historic building.

Mary, Queen of Scots is very closely associated with Holyrood. After her return from France in 1561, this striking young widow turned the Palace into a glittering residence where balls and banquets were held—much to the disapproval of John Knox, who met with her several times in Holyrood. She married her second husband, Darnley, there in 1564. Later, the Palace gained its sinister associations as the scene of the murder of David Rizzio, the Queen's secretary, whom her husband and a band of jealous and ambitious conspirators thought was gaining too much of Mary's attention.

After the mystery of Darnley's death at the Kirk o' Field, her third marriage, to Bothwell, was conducted, according to Protestant rites this time, in the Palace's great hall, demolished in the rebuilding in Charles II's time in the 17th century. Mary left Holyrood for the last time after the confrontation with her opponents, the Lords of the Congregation, on Carberry Hill. After her surrender, she briefly returned to the Palace before being led away to captivity in Loch Leven Castle in 1567.

Except when the Royal Family is in residence, most of Holyrood is today open to view. The oldest part seen by the visitor is the James V Tower, the northernmost (or left-hand) tower on the frontage—and the only surviving 16th-century part. It contains Mary's rooms on the second floor. This is the suite associated with the murder of Rizzio and a plaque marks the fatal spot. The Audience Chamber, where she argued with John Knox, retains its original panelled ceiling, while Mary's Bedroom has ceiling decoration which includes the monograms of her parents. Period furniture contributes to the atmosphere. On the floor below are Darnley's Rooms, altered in the 17th-century remodelling and featuring fine panelling, fireplaces, plasterwork and tapestries.

Along the frontage adjoining the James V Tower with the later Charles II Tower are the Duchess of Hamilton's Room and the Adam-style Royal Dining Room. Adjacent to it is the Grand Stair with its decoration of broadswords by Ferrara, the Italian craftsman. Down the southern side of the range, visitors will find the Throne Room and the Evening and Morning Drawing Rooms, chiefly used for ceremonial or social occasions. Most of the furniture is 18th-century. At the back of the Palace visitors can see three further rooms, also with fine furniture, tapestries and panelling, including the King's Bedchamber.

Another major feature is the Picture Gallery with its extraordinary collection of portraits of Scottish monarchs. They start with Fergus I in 330BC and, more than 80 portraits later, end with King James VII. Naturally, many are invented likenesses—and some are even invented monarchs—as the work was carried out by a single painter, a Dutchman, Jacob de Wet in 1684–5. This gallery was the scene of Bonnie Prince Charlie's levées during his brief occupation.

The setting for today's garden parties is in the gardens around the Palace; here also the ceremonial guards, the Royal Company of Archers, practise. A curiosity outside the Palace proper is the so-called Queen Mary's Bath House. This is a two-storey building with rubble walls dating from the 16th century, probably built as a pavilion for tennis players.

Full of historic details inside and out, the Palace of Holyroodhouse offers an insight into the turbulence of Scottish history from the early Stuart Kings to the present day.

Parliament House

High Street

Tucked inconspicuously behind the High Kirk of St Giles are the buildings associated with Scotland's own independent parliament, which last sat in 1707. The early parliaments sat in Edinburgh Castle or the Tolbooth, but Charles I proposed the building of a Parliament House in 1632. Though later extensively altered for the needs of the legal profession, the Parliament Hall still has its original hammerbeam roof; the Laigh Hall also has some original features. Its neo-classical façade, obvious from Parliament Square, is by Robert Reid.

REGISTER HOUSE

Portobello

A sailor, George Hamilton, who had seen action during the capture of the town of Puerto Bello, on the isthmus of Panama in 1739, is credited with naming Edinburgh's seaside resort. He built the first house amongst the broom and rough grasses of the empty lands between the city and Musselburgh. Then beds of clay were discovered, which rapidly led to the development of brickworks and potteries. Soon, industry and resort developments proceeded in parallel.

Though the potteries have gone, the small-scale Georgian and later Victorian resort architecture survives—as does the promenade of 1860. Bracing walks, sea air and fairground fun are still on offer at the capital's own resort.

Princes Street & The Gardens

Though for long the main shopping area in Edinburgh, Princes Street was originally intended as an elegant residential street. Its unique open atmosphere owes its existence to its early residents fighting long legal battles to ensure their views remained unspoiled by commercial developments. They secured this right by an Act of 1827. Even by this time, Princes Street was becoming a shopping concourse, though Princes Street Gardens remained private—the western gardens were laid out by 1820 and the eastern part by 1830 for the exclusive use of the residents, just as the Queen Street Gardens remain today.

However, by 1850, moves were made to make the gardens open to all—they were in any case being altered with the arrival of the railway. Today, visitors can stroll in pleasure-grounds which were once under the waters of the Nor' Loch, part of the city's defences made in 1460 by damming a stream where the North Bridge now stands. David Livingstone, explorer, Adam Black, former Lord Provost, and Allan Ramsay, poet, are some of the eminent Scots whose statues can be seen on a stroll in the gardens. The Scottish American War Memorial is also to be found there, and the popular attraction of the floral clock, just west of the Mound.

Register House

Princes Street

Considered to be a public building of the very highest architectural quality, this 'custom-built' record office by Robert Adam was started in 1774. Money from estates of Jacobite landowners forfeited after the Battle of Culloden went towards its construction. It was not finally completed till 1827 and now contains many famous documents of Scotland's history including the Scottish copy of the 1707 Treaty of Union with England. Its search rooms are open to the public.

Royal Botanic Gardens

Inverleith

A plaque in today's Waverley Station marks the site of an early 'Physic Garden', which was started at Holyrood, 1670. About a century later, it was moved to a site on Leith Walk, then finally to its present site at Inverleith in 1823. Now, more than half a million visitors annually enjoy the forward planning of earlier generations of botanists. While academic research goes on in the background, everyday visitors enjoy the 70 acres of seclusion only minutes from the city centre—and perhaps learn from the demonstration garden and exhibition hall.

Other aspects of this fine botanical assembly include the largest collection of rhododendrons in Britain, an arboretum, peat garden, woodland garden, rock and heath gardens, a magnificent herbaceous border and extensive indoor collections —from cacti and succulents, ferns and orchids, to temperate species. The low hill on which Inverleith House is built in the centre of the garden offers fine views over the greenery to the city-centre skyline.

Royal Commonwealth Pool

Only a few moments from Holyrood Park, the Royal Commonwealth Pool is a very popular facility, originally built for the Commonwealth Games in 1970. It is the city's largest swimming pool, Olympic standard, and also offers smaller pools, sauna and a fitness centre.

Royal High School

Regent Road

A school which traces its history at least to 1519, the Royal High School opened on its Calton Hill site in 1829. The building, with its outstanding neo-classical façade, was designed by Thomas Hamilton and complements the architecture of the other monuments higher up the hill. There is a good view of the school and beyond from Salisbury Crags in Holyrood Park.

The Royal High School vacated the building in 1969 and since that date conversion work has taken place to prepare it for possible political use as the venue for a Scottish Assembly.

Royal Observatory

Blackford Hill

At the Royal Observatory Visitor Centre is the largest telescope in Scotland and a range of exhibits on the theme of astronomy—as well as a fine view of Edinburgh and an astronomy bookshop. The Observatory started life on Calton Hill but was moved to a site where the air was clearer in 1895. Blackford Hill, where it now stands, is a park owned by the city since 1884 and offers fine walks by its pond and into the sheltering, tall trees of Blackford Dell.

St Giles

High Street

Once the only parish church within the Old Town walls, the High Kirk of St Giles has been greatly altered over the centuries. In 1633 it briefly acquired cathedral status. It was the setting of a famous local incident in 1637 when a town resident, Jenny Geddes, threw a stool at the preacher, who was attempting to read a newly introduced English liturgy.

Parts of the pillars below the crown spire are 12th-century, the choir dates from 1460 and the distinctive spire from 1500. The building was refaced in a smooth stone during a controversial restoration by William Burn in 1829; only the spire escaped this treatment. The most recent part is the Chapel of the Most Ancient and Most Noble Order of the Thistle, designed by Sir Robert Lorimer in 1910. Immediately behind St Giles, to the south, is Parliament Square, built over the kirkyard in which John Knox was buried.

Scott Monument

Princes Street Gardens

This unmistakable, ornately Gothic spire dominates the east end of Princes Street and is also visible from South St David Street on the west side of St Andrew Square. A monument to one of Scotland's most enduring writers, Sir Walter Scott, it is 200ft (61m) high and was built 1840–6.

SWANSTON

It was created by George Meikle Kemp, a country joiner and self-taught architect who won the open architectural competition to design a suitable memorial. (Unfortunately Kemp died by drowning in the Union Canal while his work was under construction.)

A marble statue of Scott with his dog, by Thomas Steell, sits in the centre of the monument. Today's visitors can enjoy spectacular views after climbing the 287 steps to the top.

Scottish Agricultural Museum

Ingliston

The varied farming methods of the nation's agricultural heritage—tools, equipment, photographs, plus models and displays—provide an insight into life on the land. In addition to extensive displays, fully furnished room settings give a glimpse into the former living conditions of farmers and crofters in the Lowlands and Highlands. Only a part of this wide-ranging collection is on display at any one time.

Scottish National Gallery of Modern Art

Belford Road

From its previous home in Inverleith House, in the centre of the city's Botanic Gardens, this collection was moved to the classical setting of the former John Watson's School (1823). Here the visitor can see examples of all the main forms of 20th-century art by many famous artists and sculptors, such as Hockney, Hepworth, Picasso, and Moore. There is also a fine selection of work by contemporary Scottish artists, and a changing programme of exhibitions.

Swanston

Tucked between the long slopes of the Pentlands and the encroaching suburban edges of the city and its bypass, Swanston still retains the charm and seclusion that Robert Louis Stevenson knew. The Stevensons had a summer cottage here during the 1870s and the area is mentioned in his *St Ives*; the author gleaned much material from a local shepherd. This tiny unspoilt 18th-century village is part of a conservation area and offers walks into the Pentland Hills beyond.

Tron Church

High Street

The spire of the Tron Church is a conspicuous landmark on Edinburgh's skyline, though the church itself has not been used as a place of worship since 1952. Built by 1647, its original steeple was burned down in Edinburgh's own Great Fire in 1824. The building of both North and South Bridges in the 1780s had already altered the shape of the church, as the transepts were removed or shortened to allow the bridges' construction. Now owned by the town, the church's future seems likely to involve some kind of visitor facility.

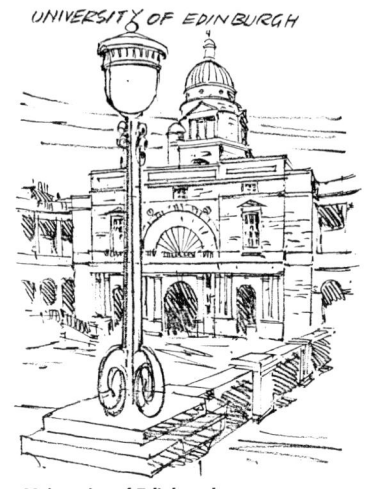

University of Edinburgh

Perhaps the most impressive of the many scattered university buildings is the Old College on South Bridge, originally designed by Robert Adam in 1789. It was not finished until 1834 since the Napoleonic Wars intervened, and then to a modified design by William Playfair. Other notable buildings include the Italianate McEwan Hall (1897) in Teviot Place and, nearby, the Venetian-style Medical School (1888).

Further university developments can be seen in the George Square area. This was originally the first residential development outside the Old Town, completed speculatively by around 1766. Sir Walter Scott's parents lived at No. 25. However, only the west side and a small portion of the east side remain of the original work.

Usher Hall

Lothian Road

Edinburgh's premier concert hall was built in 1913 with a gift of £10,000 given in 1896 by Sir John Usher, of a prominent distilling family. A grand baroque-style octagon with a copper dome, it is easily recognised by the visitor.

Water of Leith

While hardly on the same scale as the substantial rivers flowing through other Scottish towns, like the Clyde, the Tay or the Dee, nevertheless the little Water of Leith in its time helped promote many industries in Edinburgh. Rising in the Pentland Hills and entering the sea at Leith, the waters once powered corn and paper mills at Balerno, snuff mills at Currie and Juniper Green and many other commercial activities all the way to the sea. Several stretches of the river offer a 'green lung' to the city by means of walkways—pleasantly wooded and landscaped paths.

Wax Museum

High Street

Down one of the High Street's many closes, New Assembly Close, the Edinburgh Wax Museum is housed in the 1766 New Assemblies Hall, which has had a varied history. Once it hosted dancing classes, at one stage it was a Masonic Lodge which Sir Walter Scott attended, later it was used by the Commercial Bank, till 1847. Now, it contains a display of figures from Scotland's past and present, some real, some fictional—even its Chamber of Horrors has a Scottish flavour. It includes Burke and Hare, the infamous local body-snatchers.

WHITE HORSE CLOSE

West Register House

Charlotte Square

Designed by Robert Reid and originally opened in 1814 as St George's Church, the Town Council of the day intended the church to serve the inhabitants of the rapidly extending New Town. By the 1960s the problems of a dwindling congregation and need for extensive refurbishment were solved by its conversion into an extension of the nation's main record office at Register House. It became West Register House and thus the spectacular copper dome, seen from all parts of George Street, was preserved. Exhibitions in the entrance hall show some of Scotland's important historical documents.

White Horse Close

Canongate

This is a picturesque restoration, off the Canongate, of a former coaching inn and its courtyard, dating from the 17th century. The 'white horse' is said to recall a favourite palfrey of Mary, Queen of Scots. The White Horse Inn was the starting point of an early stagecoach service to London. It was also the quarters of Bonnie Prince Charlie's officers when he occupied the city during the final Jacobite rebellion in 1745. The inn and adjoining buidings are now residential property.

Pocket Guide to EDINBURGH

CITY WALKS

The Bridges and Calton Hill

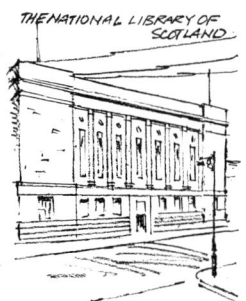

Edinburgh has several bridges which you may well cross without realising that you are actually on a bridge at all. Within a close radius of the city centre you can cross George IV Bridge, South Bridge, North Bridge and Regent Bridge. Then you are at Calton Hill which offers the best view of Edinburgh.

THE NATIONAL LIBRARY OF SCOTLAND

Allow ¾ hour. Begin at the corner of George IV Bridge and the High Street

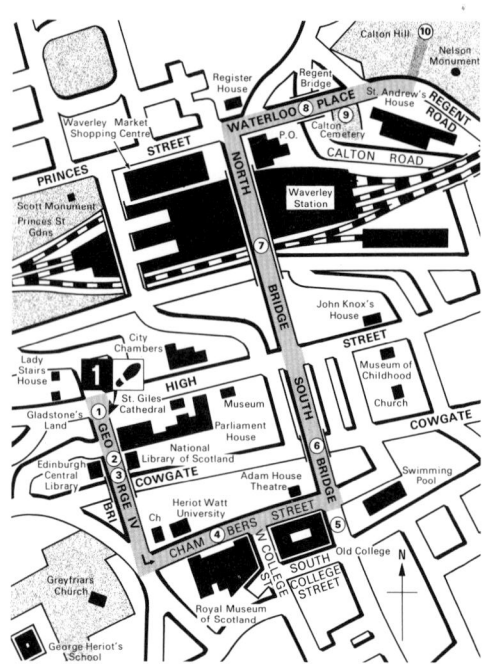

George IV Bridge ①. This bridge was designed by Thomas Hamilton and completed in 1836. Named after the king who made a historic visit in 1822, this bridge provided Edinburgh with a southern approach to the city under the 1827 Improvement Act. On this walk the first road the bridge crosses over is called the Cowgate and the second is Merchant Street.

Proceed forward and the first building on your left is the National Library of Scotland. **The National Library of Scotland** ②. Designed in 1934–6 by Reginald Failie. The steel frame was built in 1939 and the building was completed in 1950–5. There is the royal coat of arms over the front door and the tall figures on the front wall are the work of the sculptor Hew Lorimer. This library was orginally founded in 1682. Today the library has nearly 4,500,000 books and an extensive collection of manuscripts. It is one of the four largest libraries in Great Britain.

Directly across the road is Edinburgh Central Library. **Edinburgh Central Library** ③. This library has an extensive collection of reference and lending books. The Edinburgh Room is a must for visitors and locals seeking information on the city, past and present. They hold original old newspapers, maps, prints, and periodicals as well as books. Funds for the building of this library were donated to the city by the famous philanthropist, Andrew Carnegie. Designed between 1887 and 1890, the base of the building stands in the Cowgate, four storeys below.

Carry on across the bridge and take in the view of the Cowgate over the side. Turn left on to Chambers Street and on the right is the Royal Museum of Scotland. **The Royal Museum of Scotland** ④. This is one of Scotland's national institutions and the largest comprehensive museum in Europe. The range and quality of the collections are so varied that there is something to appeal to visitors of all ages and interests. The collection is housed in one of the finest Victorian buildings in the country – the visitor is immediately impressed by the main hall, which is a magnificent example of Victorian architecture.

After the Royal Museum of Scotland, keep on the same side of the road and turn right on to West College Street and then left into South College Street. At the foot of this street turn left on to South Bridge. Walk a

THE BRIDGES AND CALTON HILL

few yards and then turn left into Old College. **Old College** ⑤. The outside of the Quadrangle was designed in 1789 by Robert Adam, the famous Scottish architect, and is believed to be his greatest public work. The interior was designed by the architect William Playfair, and built between 1819 and 1827. The dome was added in 1879. The front of the building is made from Craigleith stone. The Talbot Rice Art Centre is situated in the Old College building. It houses the Torrie Collection which is a permanent display of 16th- and 17th-century European painting and sculpture and is displayed in the great gallery designed by William Playfair.

Come back into South Bridge and head further down the hill. About 200yds further on enjoy the view from this bridge on to the Cowgate. **South Bridge** ⑥. In 1785 an Act was passed authorising the building of South Bridge. It was eventually completed in 1788. The South Bridge spans the Cowgate as does George IV Bridge. At the junction of South Bridge and the High Street is the Tron Kirk where on New Year's Eve thousands of locals meet to bring in the New Year. Today South Bridge is a very busy area of the city.

On reaching the junction of South Bridge and the High Street cross straight over on to North Bridge. Continue on and stop after you pass the Scotsman offices on the left-hand side. **The North Bridge** ⑦. Beneath the bridge and stretching the full length of Princes Street to the left used to be the Old Nor' Loch, a lake which protected Edinburgh's Old Town from attack. With a city wall built around the other areas of the Old Town, Edinburgh was a well-protected capital city. The Nor' Loch took 61 years to be fully drained, from 1759 to 1820. Beneath the bridge today is Waverley Railway Station and the rest of the old loch is now Princes Street Gardens. The foundation stone for the first North Bridge was laid in October 1763 by Lord Provost Drummond. The Bridge was opened in 1769 but after only a few months a section collapsed killing five people. After several disputes about responsibility the bridge was re-opened in 1772. The present bridge dates back to 1897.

Continue to the foot of North Bridge and turn right past the Post Office until you reach Regent Bridge. **Regent Bridge** ⑧. This small bridge was designed by Archibald Elliot in 1815 and was built between 1816 and 1819. It is also a war memorial to the men who lost their lives during the Napoleonic War. The bridge carries Waterloo Place over Calton Road.

Continue along Waterloo Place until there is an entrance in to the right for Calton Cemetery. **Calton Cemetery** ⑨. The burial ground contains several interesting monuments including a statue of Abraham Lincoln, which was erected to the memory of the Scottish Americans who died during the American Civil War. To the left of Abraham Lincoln there is a circular memorial to the Scottish philosopher, David Hume. The memorial was designed by Robert Adam. The large needle-like monument in the centre of the burial ground is in memory of several political martyrs and was erected in 1844.

Leave the cemetery and turn right heading further along Waterloo Place until the junction with Regent Road. Cross the road and go up the steps leading to Calton Hill. **Calton Hill** ⑩. This is where you have one of the finest all-round views of Edinburgh. As you walk up the steps to the top of the hill, the first monument on the left is to Dugald Stewart, a professor of moral philosophy at Edinburgh University. The 12 columns form the National Monument, intended to be a replica of the Parthenon in Athens; unfortunately the subscriptions ran out and it was never completed. Calton Hill used to house Edinburgh's observatory which has now moved to Blackford Hill. The Old Observatory which remains on Calton Hill was designed by the planner of Edinburgh's New Town, James Craig. The Nelson Monument, like an upturned telescope, was designed after the Battle of Trafalgar by Robert Burn.

CALTON HILL

Greyfriars Kirkyard

Greyfriars Kirkyard has more famous people buried in it than anywhere else in Scotland. There are 56 famous Scots buried in marked graves and several others buried in unmarked graves somewhere in the Kirkyard. There is a simple route around the graves to see the headstones of some of the more famous names.

Allow about 1 hour. Begin at the entrance of Greyfriars Kirk, which is at the junction of George IV Bridge and Candlemaker Row. The first gravestone is to the famous Skye terrier dog, Greyfriars Bobby.

Greyfriars Bobby ①. Bobby was a Skye terrier who was owned by a man called John Gray, known in the town as Old Jock. After Jock died in 1858 the dog went to his graveside every day for 14 years, only leaving to get his lunch at the local tavern each day on hearing the one o'clock gun. The Lord Provost of the day presented Bobby with an inscribed collar, which, together with his dish and other items, are to be found in Huntly House Museum. Greyfriars Bobby eventually died on 14 January 1872, at the age of 16. This stone was erected by the Dog Aid Society and unveiled in 1981 by HRH The Duke of Gloucester. A bronze statue, by William Brodie, was erected near the churchyard in memory of the faithful animal.

Directly ahead of this gravestone is Greyfriars Kirk.
Greyfriars Kirk ②. The church is built on a site of a Franciscan friary (1447–1560) and was dedicated on Christmas Day 1620. It was here the National Covenant was first signed – a protest against the religious policy of Charles I. Gaelic services are still held here on Sundays at 4pm. The church was heavily restored in 1938 by Henry Kerr.

GREYFRIARS KIRK

Turn right and follow the path down the hill, parallel with Candlemaker Row, until a block of red granite stone on the left marks the front of John Gray's grave.
John Gray ③. John Gray, a local police constable, was the master of Greyfriars Bobby. He died in 1858 and was buried in a grave covered by red granite stone. The gravestone was erected by the American lovers of Bobby. Because of the dog's devotion to his master the Lord Provost presented him with a collar which signified that he was exempt from the 1867 law which required all dogs in Edinburgh to be licensed.

Continue down the hill. The last monument on the right-hand side is the Martyrs' Monument. **The Martyrs' Monument** ④. From 27 May 1661 and the execution of the Marquis of Argyll by beheading to 17 February 1688 when James Renwick was executed, 18,000 martyrs were executed in Edinburgh. Thousands of people gathered at public executions, and it is said that the roll of the execution drums was drowned out by the singing of psalms.

Turn to face away from this monument, continue forward and turn right onto the path to proceed down the hill. Follow the path which bears left and the first flat grave on the left is that of James Craig, the New Town architect. **James Craig** ⑤. Craig designed the first stage of Edinburgh's New Town. He won the competition to design a new town for Edinburgh on 17 April 1767. For his plan 23-year-old Craig was presented with a gold medal with the Freedom of the City in a silver box. His design was simple but very effective, it comprised a gridiron of broad streets with a spacious square at each end of the main street. His plan showed uniformity in the size and appearance of the houses. Sadly, he died a poor man, virtually a forgotten figure.

The next important grave is more like a small tree stump. It is situated on the grass and is marked with the initials JEM. It is the grave of James, Earl of Morton. **The Regent Morton** ⑥. James Douglas, 4th Earl of Morton (1516–81) succeeded the Earl of Mar as Regent during the childhood of James VI, the son of Mary, Queen of Scots. He held the position of Regent for six years and was influential in the building of the Half Moon Battery at Edinburgh Castle which still survives today. Morton was involved in the murder of Mary, Queen of Scots' secretary, David Rizzio, and was convicted and executed as an accessory to the murder of Mary's husband Henry, Lord Darnley.

The path now ends so you must cut over the grass to the left and head towards the stone steps. There are 10 steps in total. After the steps behind the second tree is the grave of John Porteous. **John Porteous** ⑦. He was head of Edinburgh's City Guard, the organisation which preceded the present police force. In 1736, at the execution of a smuggler called Andrew Wilson, it is said that John Porteous gave the order to his men to fire shots into the rowdy crowd. Some were killed and others injured. He was tried and sentenced to be hanged for his actions. The Edinburgh mob decided they could not wait for justice to be carried out, so they broke into the Tolbooth Prison, dragged Porteous to the Grassmarket and carried out the execution themselves. This event is now known as the Porteous Riots.

Continue forward. At the end of the path is the grave of Walter Scott. **Walter Scott** ⑧. Here lies the father of Sir Walter Scott, the famous Scottish writer and author of *Ivanhoe* and the *Waverley* novels. Walter Scott was a solicitor and writer to the Signet. His wife was Anne Rutherford and they produced 13 children, the youngest son becoming Sir Walter Scott. Unfortunately, the first children died in infancy. Walter lived in College Wynd and that was where Sir Walter was born. They were all, however, soon to move to 25 George Square.

Turn right and walk towards the gates of George Heriot's School. **George Heriot's School** ⑨. Heriot was appointed goldsmith to the king in 1601 and was known in the town by the name 'Jinglin' Geordie'. After his death in 1623 he left his fortune to the Edinburgh Town Council for the education of fatherless boys. The construction of Heriot's Hospital was started in 1628. Cromwell used it as a military hospital in 1650 but the building was not completed until 1659. In that year it accepted 30 fatherless boys. This is one of the finest buildings erected in 17th-century Scotland and still houses George Heriot's School.

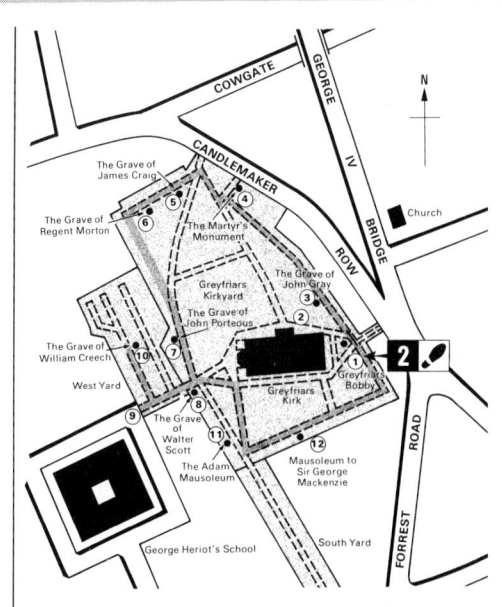

Facing away from the school gates, take the first lane on the left, which leads to the grave of William Creech. His headstone is the seventh on the right. **William Creech** ⑩. This man was Robert Burns' Edinburgh publisher and he also published the works of the Scottish economist, Adam Smith. He was Lord Provost of Edinburgh from 1811 to 1813. Creech became very rich by buying copyrights, initially for an extremely small sum. Earlier in 1788 he had been on the jury at the trial of Deacon Brodie. Brodie was a well-respected citizen by day, but by night he was a rogue, robber and gambler. Robert Louis Stevenson was later to base his story *Dr Jekyll and Mr Hyde* on Deacon Brodie.

Walk back towards the school. Turn left and leave the West Yard. Bear right and then follow the path by turning right. The last monument on the right is the large Adam Mausoleum. **The Adam Mausoleum** ⑪. Here is buried William Adam, the celebrated architect and father of two even more successful sons. His son, Robert (1728–1792), is perhaps the best known architect in the family. He designed Charlotte Square, Register House and the Old Quad at Edinburgh University.

Turn left and walk along by the back wall of the Kirkyard. The large rounded mausoleum on the right is to Sir George Mackenzie. **Sir George Mackenzie** ⑫. The prosecution of Covenanters and others accused of plotting against the king was conducted by the Lord Advocate, Sir George Mackenzie. He boasted in 1680 that he had never lost a case for the king and was known to the Covenanters as 'Bluidy Mackenzie'. In 1689 he established the Advocates' Library which is now the National Library of Scotland.

Follow the path round and it will lead to the gates, the way out of Greyfriars Kirkyard.

Cramond Village

Cramond is a peaceful 18th-century village on the outskirts of Edinburgh. The houses are huddled round the mouth of the River Almond. Cramond's harbour has a great history, stretching back through the centuries to Roman times.

CRAMOND KIRK

Allow 1 hour. Start at the point of the small headland at the mouth of the river.

The map above is for location purposes only. Cramond lies approximately six miles from the centre of Edinburgh and there are regular bus services from Princes Street (check locally for bus numbers and times). Drivers will take the A90 (Queensferry Road) from the west end of Princes Street and proceed to Cramond Road South. **Cramond Island** ①. Not far from the shore lies Cramond Island, a favourite place of Robert Louis Stevenson, author of *Treasure Island*. The island was inhabited until 1947 and can still be visited today at low tide. (Be careful not to get caught by the tide.) Across the Firth of Forth are the shores of Fife. The waters round here were once famous for their oysters.

Turn left and walk upriver until you are opposite the harbour-mouth buildings. **Cramond Harbour** ②. This peaceful harbour was once a bustling workplace. It was first used by the Romans for bringing in supplies by sea to their fort. It was later a fishing port and then an important centre for the import and export of iron goods. The buildings here have been well restored. Originally many would have been simple 'biggings' with turf roofs and earth floors.

Proceed a short distance upriver to the steps on the right-hand side. **Cramond Ferry** ③. Surely one of the shortest (and cheapest) ferry trips in Scotland. It is a voyage of about two minutes from the Cramond side of the river to the opposite bank. The ferry provides access to Dalmeny Woods and grounds, property of the Earl of Rosebery. This is a popular area for walks and picnics, particularly pretty in springtime. It is possible to continue through the Rosebery estate to South Queensferry. There is a small charge for the crossing and the ferry times are:
Summer April – September
  9am – 7pm
Winter October – March
  10am – 4pm

Continue upriver to the boatsheds on the left-hand side. **Cramond Boat Club** ④. Meet *Lucinda*, *Mairi Ruth* or *Graculus*, vessels of the Cramond Boat Club which was founded in 1934. In the winter they lie like stranded seals on the quayside; in early April a crane arrives to release them again in the river.

Follow the river to the ruined mill buildings at the weir. **Fair-A-Far Mill** ⑤. The mill dam and ruin of a forge remain beside the river. They provide a reminder of the days when there used to be five independent mills in this area. Marks on the south-west wall of the building show the position of the old mill wheel. Between 1752 and 1860 nails, shovels, hoops, chains, anchors and other iron products were manufactured here. A skilled nail maker could produce about 1,200 nails a day, earning about one shilling per week. Iron came in to Cramond from Russia and Sweden and, once transformed, the products went as far afield as Spain and the West Indies. By 1810 Cramond was no longer an important iron works, but one of the mills did continue in paper production till 1881.

Return downstream turning right, up the hill, just past Caddell's cottages. **School Brae** ⑥. At the top of School Brae, the building on the right, appropriately enough, is the Infant Department of Cramond School. On the left is the village Post Office.

At the top of School Brae turn left, and continue to Cramond Glebe Road. Turn left and go downhill to the old school house on the left. **The Old School House** ⑦. This building, now a private house, was used as a school till 1875. In 1764 it would have been ringing with the voices of 70 to 80 children who were under the guidance of the schoolmaster, Ninian Paton. This remarkable man took his post on 16 September 1764 and held his position for 52 years despite the fact that he was a heavy smoker. He had a very unusual crop growing in the school house garden as well – tobacco!

A short distance further on, turn left into the churchyard. **Cramond Kirk** ⑧. There has been a church on this site for centuries. In 1656 it was described as being in a state of 'ruinousnes'. It was repaired and the present castellated parapet was added in 1811. The present incumbent is unlikely to have the same problem as the minister in 1691 who recorded that the service was disturbed by 'ye fighting of doges in ye Church'. Locals were instructed to keep their dogs at home in future.

Turn right and walk along the edge of the graveyard to the gate in the north-east wall. **The Graveyard** ⑨. Some of the graves are almost 300 years old. Look for those with the wonderful carvings of skulls, bones and hour-glasses, all signifying death. In complete contrast are the monuments to the Cadell family, who took over the iron mills down by the river in 1771. Appropriately, they were commemorated after death not in stone but in iron.

Leave the graveyard and walk towards the house directly opposite. **Cramond House** ⑩. This is an H-plan house which dates from 1680. In its heyday it was visited by royalty. Queen Victoria visited the Duchess of Kent here before continuing her journey to her Highland home, Balmoral. The property is now owned by the Cramond Parish Church and is used as the beadle's residence.

Turn northwards towards Cramond Tower. **Cramond Tower** ⑪. This is a tall medieval defensive tower, date uncertain. One theory states that it was part of a palace belonging to the Bishop of Dunkeld. It fell into a ruinous state and the then Edinburgh Corporation began restoration work. This was suddenly halted when they realised that they didn't actually own it. It is now privately owned.

Follow the path round to the sign for the Roman camp on the left-hand side. **Roman Fort** ⑫. Started about AD142 at the instruction of Emperor Antoninus Pius this was designed to protect the eastern flank of a defensive wall which stretched across Scotland (Antonine's Wall). There is a plan showing what the fort may have looked like next to the church. It covered a full six acres and at one time was manned by more than 900 men. The walls were stone-faced barriers of clay and turf, 27ft (8m) thick. Inside the fort there were numerous facilities, including granaries, garrisons, workshops, latrines and a bath-house. Eventually these forces were pulled back behind the more famous Hadrian's Wall to the south.

This is the end of the Cramond walk. The ancient Celts called the place 'Caer Almond', which means 'fort on the Almond', hence the name by which it is still known.

CRAMOND HOUSE

The Water of Leith

Every great city has its river and Edinburgh is no exception. The Water of Leith may be much smaller than the Thames or the Seine, but in its heyday it was no less important to its city. This walk follows the river on parts of its journey through the heart of Edinburgh.

BELL'S MILL

Allow ¾ hour. Begin in front of the Granary Bar in the Dragonara Hotel.

Bell's Mill ①. The Water of Leith is approximately 22 miles (35km) long and along the river there are traces of at least 80 mills. Most of Bell's Mill was destroyed by an explosion in 1975. The remaining granary is now part of the hotel. It was the last mill on the river to be worked commercially by water. One of its products, wood flour, was used in synthetic flooring, plastics and even explosives. High above the doorway a sheaf of corn and the date 1805 recall its day as a corn mill.

Walk downhill to the river which is behind the mill. **The Water of Leith** ②. The characteristic brown tinge to the water comes from the peaty moorlands where it originates. The water quality is good and the river supports a population of trout throughout its course. In 1617 Leith water entered the law books. An Act of Scots Parliament stated that the Standard Pint Jug should contain, 'Three pounds seven ounces troy of clear running water of the Water of Leith'.

Walk downstream to the bridge. **Belford Bridge** ③. This bridge was constructed between 1885 and 1887. The new walkway goes right underneath it. On the left-hand pier of the bridge it is possible to make out the City of Edinburgh's coat of arms. On the opposite side of the same pier is the Scottish royal coat of arms. The faintly visible motto is, *Nemo me impune lacessit*, 'No one shall attack me with impunity'.

Follow the path through the trees as far as the steps going up the river bank. **Sunbury** ④. The new houses along the opposite river bank are part of the Sunbury development. They take their name from the Sunbury Distillery which stood in this area. Also nearby was a tannery called the Leggate Skinworks. The large sheds on the opposite bank store wood for the Whytock and Reid Company whose cabinet factory was built by the river in 1886.

Climb the steps, turn right and proceed downhill to the centre of the old Dean Bridge. **Dean Village** ⑤. The word 'dene' or 'dean' means deep valley, but originally this picturesque area was known as the 'Village of the Water of Leith'. It grew up around the mills that had been here since the 12th century. At one time it was the centre of a community of baxters (bakers) who operated 11 watermills along the river and two granaries in the area. Upstream on the right-hand side is the old school, now converted into flats. Opposite it, downstream, is the massive West Mill. Rebuilt in 1805, it is the largest surviving industrial building of its era. In the distance the Holy Trinity Church can be seen rising above the trees. It is no longer used but is preserved as an electricity sub-station.

Cross the bridge to the doorway opposite at the bottom of Bell's Brae. **Baxters' Tolbooth** ⑥. This 17th-century building was the headquarters and granary of the Incorporation of Baxters (bakers). The carving over the doorway shows two baker's peels (shovels). On the peels are three cakes and a pie. The inscriptions read, 'God's providence is our inheritance' and 'God Bless the Baxters of Edinburgh who built this house in 1675'. The steep hill or 'brae' was once a main road out of Edinburgh. James Boswell and Dr Johnson clattered down it on their journey to the Hebrides.

From the Tolbooth turn left down Miller Row to the three mill stones set in the roadway. **Lindsay's Mill** ⑦. This mill was situated virtually on top of the damhead which can still be glimpsed through the railings. Listening to the water roar, it is strange to

THE WATER OF LEITH 71

THE WATER OF LEITH

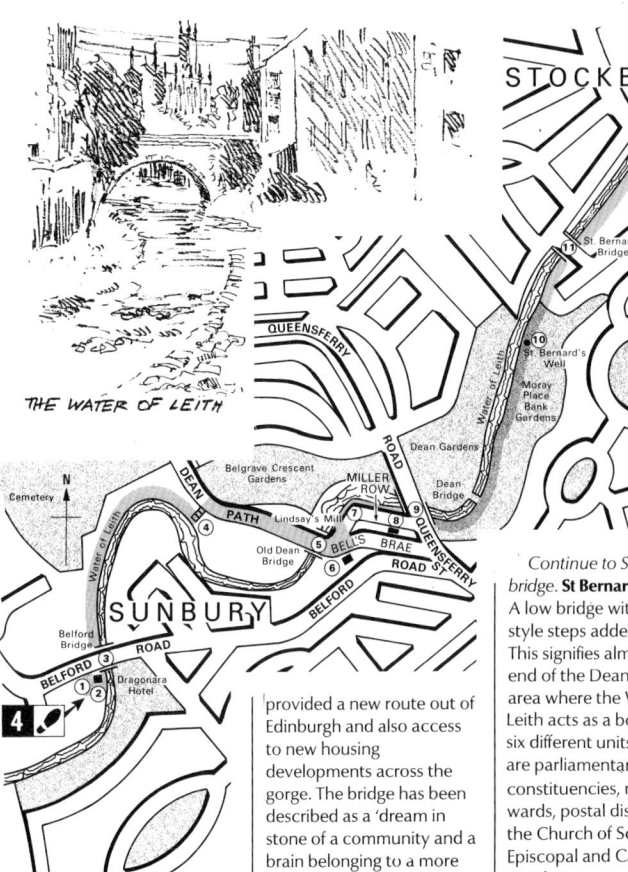

think that in 1978 the Water of Leith was disappearing. Between Belford and Dean Bridges gallons of water were vanishing through the river bed. The cause is still a mystery.

Follow the path until you are opposite the Oxylitre building. **Mar's Mill** ⑧. Mar's Mill originally stood on this site. The present neo-baronial building was erected by a publisher in 1912 as a racquets court. Today it is the home of Oxylitre, makers of anaesthetic and oxygen therapy equipment.

Walk underneath the bridge. **Dean Bridge** ⑨. Constructed in 1832 by the famous Scottish engineer, Thomas Telford, the bridge provided a new route out of Edinburgh and also access to new housing developments across the gorge. The bridge has been described as a 'dream in stone of a community and a brain belonging to a more gracious age'. It is 106ft (32m) high and cost £18,556 to build. The masonry piers are hollow and are regularly inspected. The raised parapet is the result of a report in 1886 on the 'Prevention of suicides at Dean Bridge'.

Take the path along the river to the circular Roman temple. **St Bernard's Well** ⑩. In the 1800s the mineral waters here were very popular. The temple was originally built by a wealthy law lord who felt he had benefited from the waters. It was restored in 1888. The statue is of Hygeia, health personified. St Bernard's was not popular with everyone; a man called Forsyth in 1805 commented that 'this spring has a slight resemblance in flavour to the washings of a foul gun barrel'.

Continue to St Bernard's bridge. **St Bernard's Bridge** ⑪. A low bridge with Jacobean style steps added in 1887. This signifies almost the end of the Dean Gorge, an area where the Water of Leith acts as a boundary for six different units; these are parliamentary constituencies, municipal wards, postal districts and the Church of Scotland, Episcopal and Catholic parishes.

Go underneath the bridge, turn right and follow the river to the traffic lights. **Stockbridge** ⑫. Another of the string of industrial villages along the river which at one time provided the city with foodstuffs, paper, leather, spices, snuff, glue, spirits, beer, rope, flax and wood, among other things. The road to the right leads up to the town centre. It leaves behind a river that has given much to the city and is still close to the hearts of many Edinburgh citizens – especially those of the Water of Leith Trust, founded in 1976. It is encouraging to know that they are slowly transforming what Robert Louis Stevenson called 'that dirty Water of Leith' into something very beautiful.

Princes Street

The view of Edinburgh Castle from Princes Street is magnificent and Princes Street Gardens, which run parallel to the main street, are a joy to walk through. Princes Street is today the main shopping centre of Edinburgh.

> Allow ¾ hour. Begin at the corner of North Bridge and Princes Street outside the main entrance to the North British Hotel.

The North British Hotel ①. This hotel was designed by William Hamilton Beattie in a competition of 1895 and was opened in October 1902. The large clock tower is 190ft (58m) high and is one of Edinburgh's familiar landmarks. The clock is always 3 minutes fast so that people heading to the adjacent railway station will arrive in plenty of time for their train.

Opposite this hotel is Register House. **Register House** ②. This was the first important government building in the UK. Designed by Robert Adam, it is probably the finest classical building in Edinburgh. The foundation stone was laid on 27 June 1774. Register House stores Scotland's national records and it is often used by visitors tracing their Scottish ancestry. Outside the front of this building there is a bronze statue of the Duke of Wellington on his horse, Copenhagen. The statue was designed by Sir John Steell and is known as the Iron Duke in bronze by Steell.

Proceed along Princes Street. On the left, after the North British Hotel, is Waverley Market. **The Waverley Market** ③. Directly above the Waverley Station, here is a good speciality shopping centre under one roof. There are many small, quality retailers specialising mainly in fashion and foods, including beauty products, jewellery, perfumes, knitwear and leather goods. The City of Edinburgh Tourist Information Centre is also situated here on street level. It provides a complete tourist and accommodation service for visitors to the capital.

Continue along the main street and cross Waverley Bridge on the left-hand side.

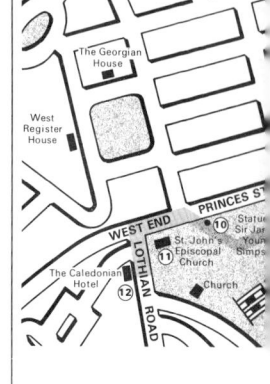

THE NATIONAL GALLERY

Standing inside Princes Street Gardens there is a statue of David Livingstone. **David Livingstone** ④. David Livingstone was made an honorary Burgess of Edinburgh in 1857. Born in March 1813, he became a missionary and was sent to Africa, where he crossed the Kalahari Desert, went up the Zambesi River and discovered the Victoria Falls. In 1865, Livingstone went in search of the sources of the Nile. He went missing for five years but was found safely by an American newspaper correspondent. When he died in May 1873, the nation mourned the loss.

Continue along Princes Street. The next tall monument on the left is the Scott Monument. **The Scott Monument** ⑤. A monument to Sir Walter Scott, designed by George Meikle Kemp and built between 1840 and 1844. It takes the style of an elaborate Gothic spire and it is more than 200ft (61m) high. You can reach the top by walking up the 287 steps. The exterior of the monument is decorated with figures from Scottish history and characters from Scott's novels. In the centre is the marble statue of Sir Walter Scott with his dog, Maida, by his side.

Directly across the road is the famous department

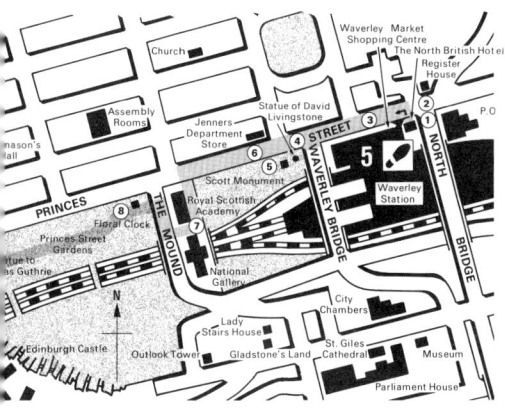

store, Jenners. **Jenners Department Store** ⑥. This store is Edinburgh's equivalent of Harrods of London. The building was designed by William Hamilton Beattie in 1895 and is typical of a large Victorian store. When built this was one of the biggest department stores in Britain.

Proceed along Princes Street to the junction with the Mound where there are two large gallery buildings. On Princes Street is the Royal Scottish Academy and at the rear of this building is the National Gallery of Scotland. **The Royal Scottish Academy/The National Gallery** ⑦. The RSA, on Princes Street, was designed by William Playfair and was completed in 1826. It was enlarged between 1833 and 1836. Above the portico entrance is a large statue of Queen Victoria, designed by John Steell. The National Gallery is also by William Playfair and is one of the more important of the smaller galleries of Europe. As well as paintings by Scotland's finest artists, works by masters such as Rubens, Turner and Gainsborough also hang here.

Cross the Mound and enter West Princes Street at the Floral Clock. **The Floral Clock** ⑧. This is the oldest Floral Clock in the world, built in 1903. The statue beside the clock is of the Scottish poet, Allan Ramsay, writer of the religious satire *The Gentle Shepherd*. He opened in Edinburgh what is believed to be the oldest circulating library in Britain.

Walk through the Princes Street Gardens and pass a statue on the right-hand side, to the Royal Scots Greys and, on the left, the Ross Band Stand. Continue until, on the right-hand side, you reach a statue to Thomas Guthrie. **Thomas Guthrie** ⑨. Guthrie was a Church of Scotland minister who organised non-sectarian schools for poor children. He gained world-wide fame and his caring establishments became known as the 'Ragged Schools'. His knowledge of drunkenness among the poor led him to fight for control of the supply of liquor. He was one of the men responsible for the passing of the 1853 Act which cut back the opening hours of public houses and closed them completely on a Sunday.

Carry on straight ahead until you reach some steps which lead back on to the main street. On reaching the street you will see, directly on the right, a statue to Sir James Young Simpson. **Sir James Young Simpson** ⑩. This statue was designed by William Brodie in 1877. Sir James Young Simpson was born in Bathgate but he studied at Edinburgh University, starting his course at the age of 14. In 1847 he made the amazing discovery of the anaesthetic properties of chloroform. Simpson inspired such confidence in his discovery that Queen Victoria used chloroform at the birth of Prince Leopold in 1853. He became a Baronet in 1866.

Continuing towards the West End, reach St John's Episcopal Church on the left. **St John's Episcopal Church** ⑪. This church is dated 1815–18 and was designed by William Burn. The cost of building it was £18,000, raised by Bishop Sandford from donations and an issue of shares. Burn's interior has been described as a masterpiece of its time. There is a convenient café in the basement of the church. The Scottish portrait painter, Raeburn, is buried in the mortuary chapel at the east end.

Turn left at the end of the church on to Lothian Road. You now see the large Caledonian Hotel. **The Caledonian Hotel** ⑫. This is one of the largest and most distinguished of Edinburgh's principal buildings. It opened for the first time in December 1903 and soon became one of the great railway hotels of Britain. Distinguished guests who have stayed here include Charlie Chaplin, Laurel and Hardy, Ginger Rogers, Marlon Brando, Bob Hope and Bing Crosby. Even Roy Rogers and his 'wonder horse' Trigger stayed here.

THE SCOTT MONUMENT

The New Town

In 1767, James Craig a 23-year-old architect, won the competition to design a new town for Edinburgh. His simple but effective plan produced two fine squares and wide Georgian streets of extreme elegance. Today the New Town has some of the finest Georgian architecture in the whole of Europe.

CHARLOTTE SQUARE

Allow 1 hour. Start at the corner of South Charlotte Street and Charlotte Square at the house of Alexander Graham Bell.

Alexander Graham Bell ①. The inventor of the telephone was born here at 16 South Charlotte Street on 3 March 1847. He attended the Royal High School and then left for London and the USA. It was while he was Professor of Vocal Physiology at Boston University that he invented the telephone. He patented the idea in 1876.

Turn left into Charlotte Square. On the right, in the centre of the square, is a statue of Prince Albert on horseback. **Prince Albert** ②. This statue was designed by John Steell and unveiled by Queen Victoria. She was so delighted with the statue that she called John Steell to Holyrood Palace and, on the same day, made him Sir John Steell. Queen Victoria and Prince Albert first visited Edinburgh in 1842. This visit was an embarrassment to the authorities as the Lord Provost, Sir James Forrest,

WEST REGISTER HOUSE

overslept and failed to meet the Queen at the correct time.

Continue forward. On the corner of Charlotte Square and Hope Street, above No 24, is the house where Douglas Haig was born. **Douglas Haig** ③. The first Earl Haig was born in Edinburgh in 1861. In 1883 he went to Sandhurst and then travelled to India with the British army. He was a brigade major during the Boer War. After service in Egypt, South Africa and India he became Commander-in-Chief at the start of World War I. It is believed that some of his orders committed the lives of many of his soldiers when there was little chance of success. Also related to Earl Haig are the founders of the famous whisky distilling firm, and Alexander Haig, the former American Secretary of State.

Continue to walk round the square. The tall building on the left is West Register House. **West Register House** ④. This was formerly St George's Church, designed by Robert Reid and founded in 1811. It has been converted into a modern record repository which opened in 1971. It contains modern government records including the Scottish Railway archives, business archives, maps and plans. The Scottish Record Office Museum in the front hall contains a permanent exhibition of historic Scottish documents.

Continue around the square to Nos 1–11, a block

THE NEW TOWN 75

of buildings designed by Robert Adam. **Nos 1–11 Charlotte Square** ⑤. This square provides the visitor with some of the finest Georgian architecture in the whole of Europe. No 1 has one of the best Georgian interiors in Edinburgh. No 5 is the headquarters of the National Trust for Scotland and No 6 is the official residence of the Secretary of State for Scotland. Meanwhile No 7 is the Georgian House, a superb Georgian-style house which is open to the public and is run by the National Trust. Between No 8 and No 9 there is a plaque on the wall recording that Lord Lister stayed here from 1870 to 1877. He was the pioneer of the carbolic spray as an antiseptic.

Leave Charlotte Square by George Street. Walk along George Street and turn left into North Castle Street. On the right at No 39 is the house which used to belong to Sir Walter Scott. **Sir Walter Scott** ⑥. He stayed at No 39 Castle Street periodically from 1802 to 1826. Born at the top of College Wynd, during his childhood he contracted polio. He was educated at the Royal High School and Edinburgh University. His first important literary work was *The Minstrelsy of the Scottish Border*. His later works include *Ivanhoe* and *Rob Roy* as well as the *Waverley* novels and the famous poem *The Lady of the Lake*. Sir Walter was created a Baronet in 1820 by George IV.

Carry on down the hill and turn right on to Queen Street. At No 51, on the right-hand side, there is the old house of Sir James Young Simpson. **Sir James Young Simpson** ⑦. He stayed here in Queen Street for some time. It was he who discovered the anaesthetic properties of chloroform. Ether was discovered in America in 1846 and Simpson's discovery came in 1847. Chloroform became widely accepted after Queen Victoria used it during the birth of Prince Leopold. Having been made physician to the Queen of Scotland in 1847, Simpson was created a Baronet in 1866.

Continue along Queen Street and turn left into Frederick Street which is flanked on each side by Queen Street Gardens. Then turn right on to Heriot Row. At No 17 is the house of Robert Louis Stevenson. **Robert Louis Stevenson** ⑧. The author of well-known stories such as *Treasure Island*, *Kidnapped* and *The Strange Case of Dr Jekyll and Mr Hyde*. The Jekyll and Hyde tale may be based on a real Edinburgh character called Deacon Brodie who by day was a well-respected citizen but by night was a rogue, gambler and robber.

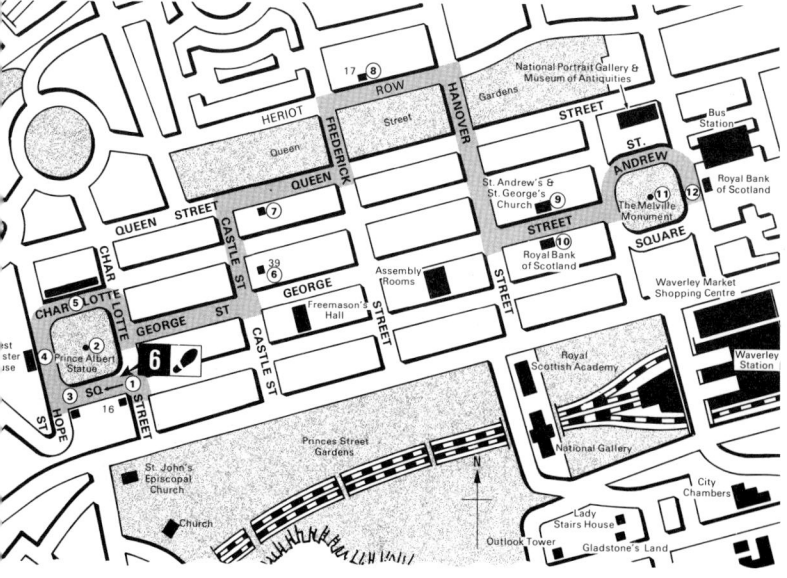

THE NEW TOWN

In France, Stevenson married an American lady called Fanny Osbourne and was to travel to Tahiti, Hawaii and Samoa, where he died in 1894. *Treasure Island* is indeed a world-renowned story of high adventure.

Move along to Heriot Row and turn right on to Hanover Street. Walk to the top of this street and turn left on to George Street. After the George Hotel on the left there is St Andrew's and St George's Church. **St Andrew's and St George's Church** ⑨. This church was built to an oval design by Major Andrew Fraser and was opened for the first time in 1784. This was the first burgh church in the New Town and was named after Scotland's patron saint. The 168ft steeple was erected three years after the main building was built. The interior supports a superb Adam-style ceiling. One authority described the ceiling as 'one of the small masterpieces of 18th-century Edinburgh'.

Directly opposite the church is the fine building of the Royal Bank of Scotland. **The Royal Bank of Scotland** ⑩. In 1843 the directors of this bank purchased for £20,000 a building on this site which was the Royal College of Physicians and promptly razed it to the ground. The bank then built the present building on the site to the design of David Rhind. The foundation stone was laid on 4 June 1844 and the office opened for business in April 1847.

Continue along George Street and reach St Andrew Square. In the centre is the large monument to Henry Dundas, the 1st Viscount Melville. **The Melville Monument** ⑪. This monument was erected in 1823 in memory of Henry Dundas the 1st Viscount Melville (1742–1811). He was a dominant figure in politics and for over four decades he was treasurer to the Navy and Lord Advocate and Keeper to the Scottish Signet. The subscription for the monument was raised by members of the Royal Navy. It was designed by William Burn and the statue is by Chantrey.

Walk around the square and at its head, set back from the street, is another fine bank building, the Royal Bank of Scotland. Notice the out-of-proportion statue at the front of the building. **The Royal Bank of Scotland** ⑫. This building was at one time a splendid Georgian town house and was erected between 1772 and 1774 for Sir Lawrence Dundas. The site was originally intended for St Andrew's and St George's Church, which was relegated to nearby George Street. Today it is the registered office of the Royal Bank of Scotland. Built of Ravelston stone, the house was designed by Sir William Chambers RA. Today's splendid banking hall was added in 1858 with its magnificent dome pierced by 120 stars. This section was designed by Peddie and Kinnear of Edinburgh who also designed the charmingly decorated staircase and probably the two-storeyed entrance hall. This fine building is where the walk ends.

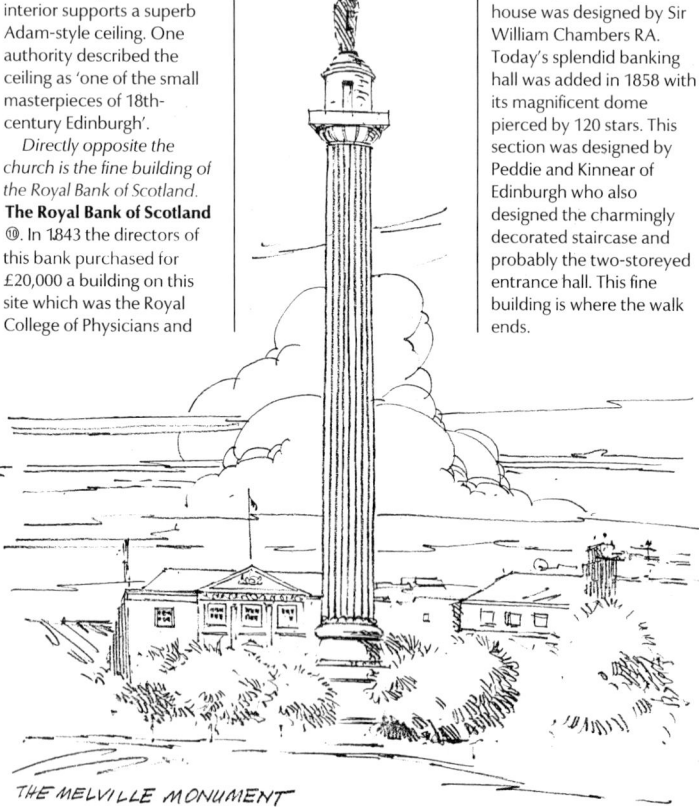

THE MELVILLE MONUMENT

Pocket Guide to EDINBURGH

- Using the Directory 78
- How to Get There 79
- Accommodation 79
- Eating and Drinking Out 81
- Places to Visit 81
- Entertainment 85
- Recreation and Sport 86
- Shopping 88
- Transport 89
- Useful Information 90

DIRECTORY

Using the directory

ABBREVIATIONS

AM	Ancient Monuments in Scotland are the responsibility of the Scottish Development Department, 3–11 Melville St, Edinburgh EH3 7QD. Membership of the Friends of the Scottish Monuments can be purchased from the above address.
BH	Bank Holidays
ch 15 20p	children under 15 20p
ch 20p	children 20p
ER	Egon Ronay
Etr	Easter
ex	Except
Free	Admission free
NTS	National Trust for Scotland
Pen	Senior Citizens
PH	Public Holidays

TELEPHONE NUMBERS

There is no need to dial 031 when telephoning within Edinburgh.

AA CLASSIFICATIONS

Hotels

★	Good hotels and inns, generally of small scale and with good furnishings and facilities.
★★	Hotels with a higher standard of accommodation. There should be 20% private bathrooms or showers.
★★★	Well-appointed hotels. Two-thirds of the bedrooms should have private bathrooms or showers.
★★★★	Exceptionally well-appointed hotels offering high standards of comfort and service. All bedrooms should have private bathrooms or showers.
★★★★★	Luxury hotels offering the highest international standards.

Restaurants

×	Modest but good restaurant.
××	Restaurant offering a higher standard of comfort than above.
×××	Well-appointed restaurant.
××××	Exceptionally well-appointed restaurant.
×××××	Luxury restaurant.

Rosettes

The rosette award is used to high-light hotels and restaurants where it is judged that the food and service can be especially recommended.

❀	The food is of a higher standard than is expected for its classification.
❀❀	Excellent food and service, irrespective of its classification.
❀❀❀	Outstanding food and service, irrespective of its classification.

Camping and caravanning sites

▶	Site licence, 10% of pitches for touring units; site density not more than 30 per acre; 2 separate toilets for each sex per 30 pitches; good quality tapwater; efficient waste disposal; regular cleaning of ablutions block; fire precautions; well-drained ground.
▶▶	All one-pennant facilities plus: 2 washbasins with hot and cold water for each sex per 30 pitches in separate washrooms; warden available at certain times of the day.
▶▶▶	All two-pennant facilities plus: one shower or bath for each sex per 30 pitches, with hot and cold water; electric shaver points and mirrors; all-night lighting of toilet blocks; deep sinks for washing clothes; facilities for buying milk, bread and gas; warden in attendance by day, on call by night.
▶▶▶▶	All three-pennant facilities plus: a higher degree of organisation than one–three pennant sites;

The information in this Directory is liable to change at short notice. While every effort has been made to ensure that it is comprehensive and up to date, the publishers cannot accept responsibility for errors or omissions, or for changes in the details given.

DIRECTORY

attention to landscaping; reception office; late-arrivals enclosure; first-aid hut; shop; routes to essential facilities lit after dark; play area; bad-weather shelter; hard standing for touring vans.

For more details on the accommodation and eating out establishments listed, please see the current edition of the AA guides: *Hotels and Restaurants in Britain*; *Guesthouses, Farmhouses and Inns in Britain* and *Holiday Homes, Cottages and Apartments in Britain*, and the Egon Ronay Guides: *Healthy Eating Out*; *Pub Guide*; *Just a Bite* and *Egon Ronay's Guide to Hotels, Restaurants and Inns*.

How to get there

AIR SERVICES

Planes fly to and from Edinburgh from the following airports

London:
Gatwick – British Caledonian; Heathrow – British Airways, British Midland; Stansted – Air UK

Other UK airports:
Birmingham – British Airways; East Midlands – Air Ecosse; Glasgow – British Airways; Isle of Man – Manx Airlines; Manchester – Loganair, British Airways; Newquay – British Airways, Brymon Airlines; Norwich – Air UK; Plymouth – British Airways, Brymon Airlines; Wick (Highland) – Loganair, Air Ecosse

Channel Islands
Guernsey – Guernsey Airlines; Jersey – British Airways, Guernsey Airlines

Ireland:
Belfast – Loganair; Cork – British Airways and Aer Lingus

BRITISH RAIL

Frequent Inter City express trains run daily from **King's Cross Station** in London to Edinburgh, the journey takes approximately 5 hours.

There is also an Inter City Motorail service that operates regularly from **Euston**, London, to Edinburgh.

COACH SERVICES

National Express operate a network of express coach services throughout England and Wales and into Scotland from local coach and bus stations.

Cotter Coachline and Scottish City Link operate motorway express services from Victoria Coach Station in London. The journey time is approximately 8 hours.

Cotter Coachline 298 Regent Street, London W1R 6LE (no personal callers) 01-930 5781

Scottish City Link 298 Regent Street, London W1R 6LE 01-636 9373

BY ROAD

There are no problems with road access to Edinburgh. It can be approached from the south-east via the A1, A697 and A68; from the south-west via the M6, A74 and A702; from Glasgow via the M8 and A8; from Stirling via the M9 and A8; and from Perth and the north via the A9, M90 and the Forth Bridge.

Accommodation

HOTELS—The AA's choice

★★★★★ **Caledonian**
Princes St (Pride of Britain) 031-225 2433 Telex no 72179

★★★★ **Carlton Highland**
North Bridge (Scottish Highland) 031-556 7277 Telex no 727001

★★★★ **George** George St 031-225 1251 Telex no 72570

★★★★ **Ladbroke Dragonara** Bells Mill, 69 Belford Rd (Ladbroke) 031-332 2545 Telex no 727979

★★ **Albany** 39–43 Albany St 031-556 0397 Telex no 727079

★★★ **Barnton Thistle**
Queensferry Rd (Thistle) 031-339 1144 Telex no 727928

★★★ **Braid Hills** 134 Braid Rd, Braid Hills (2½m S A702) 031-447 8888 Telex no 72311

★★★ **Bruntsfield** 69–74 Bruntsfield Pl (Best Western) 031-229 1393 Telex no 727897

★★★ **Crest** Queensferry Rd (Crest) 031-332 2442 Telex no 72541

★★★ **Donmaree** 21 Mayfield Gdns 031-667 3641

★★★ **Ellersly House** 4 Ellersly Rd (Embassy) 031-337 6888 Telex no 76357

★★★ **Howard** Great King St 031-557 3500 Telex no 727887

★★★ **King James Thistle** 107 St James Centre (Thistle) 031-556 0111 Telex no 727200

★★★ **Old Waverley** Princes St (Scottish Highland) 031-556 4648 Telex no 727050

★★★ **Post House**
Corstorphine Rd (Trusthouse Forte) 031-334 8221 Telex no 727103

★★★ **Roxburghe**
Charlotte Sq (Best Western) 031-225 3921 Telex no 727054

DIRECTORY

★★★Royal Scot 111 Glasgow Rd (Swallow) 031-334 9191 Telex no 727197

★★★Stakis Commodore West Marine Dr, Cramond Foreshore (Stakis) 031-336 1700 Telex no 727167

★★★Stakis Grosvenor Grosvenor St (Stakis) 031-226 6001 Telex no 72445

★★Clarendon Grosvenor St (Scottish Highland) 031-337 7033 Telex no 78215

★★Harp St John's Rd, Corstorphine (3½m W on A8) (Osprey) 031-334 4750

★★Iona Strathearn Pl 031-447 6264

★★Murrayfield 18 Corstorphine Rd (Alloa) 031-337 1844

★★Suffolk Hall 10 Craigmillar Pk 031-667 9328

Capital (awaiting inspection) Clermiston Rd 031-334 3391

OTHER RECOMMENDED HOTELS (ER)

Edinburgh Sheraton 1 Festival Sq 031-229 9131 Telex no 72398

GUESTHOUSES

Adam Hotel 19 Lansdowne Cres 031-337 1148. Closed Xmas & New Year

Adria Hotel 11–12 Royal Ter 031-556 7875. Closed Dec

Allison House 15/17 Mayfield Gdns 031-667 8049. Closed Xmas & New Year

Ben Doran Hotel 11 Mayfield Gdns 031-667 8488. Closed 20–27 Dec

Boisdale Hotel 9 Coates Gdns 031-337 1134

Bonnington 202 Ferry Rd 031-554 7610

Brunswick 7 Brunswick St 031-556 1238

Buchan Hotel 3 Coates Gdns 031-337 1045

Clans Hotel 4 Magdala Cres 031-337 6301

Dorstan Private Hotel 7 Priestfield Rd 031-667 6721. Closed 2 wks Xmas

Dunstane House 4 West Coates 031-337 6169. Closed Xmas–4 Jan

Galloway 22 Dean Park Cres 031-332 3672 Telex no 72165

Glenisla Hotel 12 Lygon Rd 031-667 4098

Greenside Hotel 9 Royal Ter 031-557 0022. Open Jan–Oct

Grosvenor 1 Grosvenor Gdns, Haymarket 031-337 4143

Halcyon Hotel 8 Royal Ter 031-556 1033. Closed Feb & New Year

Heriott Park 256 Ferry Rd 031-552 6628

Hillview 92 Dalkeith Rd 031-667 1523

Kariba 10 Granville Ter 031-229 3773

Kildonan Lodge Hotel 27 Craigmillar Pk 031-667 2793

Kingsley 30 Craigmillar Pk 031-667 8439

Kirtle House 8 Minto St 031-667 2813

Lindsay 108 Polwarth Ter 031-337 1580

Marchhall Hotel 14–16 Marchhall Cres 031-667 2743

Marvin 46 Pilrig St 031-554 6605

Newington 18 Newington Rd 031-667 3356

Ravensdown 248 Ferry Rd 031-552 5438

Rockville Hotel 2 Joppa Pans, Joppa 031-669 5418

St Bernards 22 St Bernards Cres 031-332 2339

St Margaret's 18 Craigmillar Pk 031-667 2202

Salisbury Hotel 45 Salisbury Rd 031-667 1264

Sherwood 42 Minto St 031-667 1200. Closed Xmas & New Year

Southdown 20 Craigmillar Pk 031-667 2410

Thrums Private Hotel 14 Minto St 031-667 5545. Closed Xmas & New Year

Tiree 26 Craigmillar Pk 031-667 7477

CAMPING AND CARAVANNING

▶▶▶▶Mortonhall Caravan Park (NT265680) 30 Frogston Rd East. Signposted. 031-664 1533. Open 28 Mar–Oct, booking advisable Jun–Aug

▶▶▶▶Drum Mohr Caravan Park (NT373734) Levenhall, Musselburgh. Signposted. 031-665 6867. Open Mar–Oct, booking advisable Jul & Aug

▶▶▶Little France Caravan Park (NT289704) 219 Old Dalkeith Rd. Signposted. 031-664 4742. Open Apr–Oct, booking advisable Jul & Aug

---

SELF-CATERING

Controller of Catering & Residences, Heriot-Watt University Riccarton, Currie, Edinburgh EH14 4AS. 031-449 5111 ext 2178. Self-contained flatlets on the University Campus, for 3–6 persons. 2 Jul–24 Sep

Keyplan Apartments Linton Court, Murieston Rd, Edinburgh EH11 2JJ. 031-337 4040. Forty-two units within a newly developed block of flats for 1–7 persons. Open all year

Pollock Halls of Residence 18 Holyrood Park Rd, Edinburgh EH16 5AY. 031-667 1971. Student flats, within halls of residence, for 1–5 persons. Open 2 Jul–24 Sep

---

YOUTH HOSTELS

(Not AA-appointed accommodation). Low-priced accommodation for members of the Youth Hostels Association. Membership can be obtained from any hostel.

Scottish Youth Hostels Association 161 Warrender Park Rd 031-229 8660

Edinburgh Bruntsfield Youth Hostel 7 Bruntsfield Cres 031-447 2994

Edinburgh Eglinton Youth Hostel 18 Eglinton Cres 031-337 1120

YMCA Princes St 031-225 1174

YWCA Randolph Pl 031-225 4379

Eating and Drinking Out

(ER indicates Egon Ronay–appointed establishments)

RESTAURANTS – The AA's choice

×× **Alp-Horn** 167 Rose St 031-225 4787. Closed Sun, Mon, 2 wks from Xmas Eve & 3 wks end June/beginning Jul. Swiss cooking

×× **L'Auberge** 56 St Mary's St 031-556 58888. French cooking

×× **Champany Inn Town** 2 Bridge Rd, Colinton 031-441 2587. Steak restaurant

×× **Lancers Brasserie** 5 Hamilton Pl, Stockbridge 031-332 3444. North Indian & Bengali cooking

×× **Lightbody's** 123 Glasgow Rd 031-334 2300. Closed Sun. British & French cooking

×× **Martins** 70–72 Rose St, North Ln 031-225 3106. Closed Sun, Mon, 26 Dec–3 Jan & 2 wks Jun/Jul. Lunch not served Sat. Scottish, French & Italian cooking

×× **Ristorante Milano** 7 Victoria St 031-226 5260. Closed Sun. Italian cooking

× **Chez Julie** 110 Raeburn Pl 031-332 2827. Closed Sun. French cooking

× **Kalpna** 2–3 St Patrick Sq 031-667 9890. Closed Sun. Indian vegetarian cooking

× **Kweilin Cantonese** 19–21 Dundas St 031-557 1875. Closed 25 Dec, 1 Jan & Chinese New Year. Cantonese cooking

× **MacKintosh's** 24A Stafford St 031-226 7530. Closed Sun, 26, 27 Dec & 1, 2 Jan. Lunch not served Sat. Scottish & French cooking

× **New Edinburgh Rendezvous** 10A Queensferry St 031-225 2023. Closed 25, 26 Dec, 1 Jan & Chinese New Year. Chinese cooking

× **Shamiana** 14 Brougham St 031-228 2265. Closed 25 Dec & 1 Jan. Lunch not served. Kashmiri & North Indian cooking

× **Verandah Tandoori** 17 Dalry Rd 031-337 5828. Bengali & North Indian cooking

OTHER RECOMMENDED RESTAURANTS (ER)

Caledonian Hotel, Pompadour Restaurant Princes St 031-225 2433. Closed 26 Dec & 2 Jan. Lunch not served Sat & Sun. French & Scottish cooking

Donmaree Hotel Restaurant 21 Mayfield Gdns 031-667 3641. Closed Sun & BH. Lunch not served Sat. French cooking

No 10 10 Melville Pl 031-225 8727. Lunch not served Sun; dinner not served Sun in winter.

LIGHT MEALS AND SNACKS (ER)

Brasserie Saint Jacques King James Thistle Hotel, Leith St 031-556 0111. Closed 25 & 26 Dec

Handsel's Wine Bar 22 Stafford St 031-225 5521. Closed Sun, BH & first wk Jan

Helios Fountain 7 Grassmarket 031-229 7884. Closed Sun, 25, 26 Dec & 1, 2 Jan

Henderson's Salad Table 94 Hanover St 031-225 2131. Closed Sun (except during Festival) & BH

Laigh Kitchen 117a Hanover St 031-225 1552. Closed Sun & some BH

Sunflower Country Kitchen 4 South Charlotte St 031-220 1700. Closed Sun, 25, 26 Dec & 1, 2 Jan

Waterfront Wine Bar 1c Dock Pl, Leith 031-554 7427. Closed Sun, 25 & 26 Dec, 1, 2 Jan

PUB FOOD (ER)

Cramond Inn Cramond Glebe Rd, Cramond 031-336 2035. Scottish and traditional bar food is served here, but at lunchtime only

Places to Visit

CITY CENTRE

Brass Rubbing Centre Canongate Tolbooth, 163 Canongate, Royal Mile 031-225 2424 ext 6638. Open Jun–Sep Mon–Sat 10–6; Oct–May Mon–Sat 10–5. Also open Sun during Festival. (Charge for rubbing facilities)

Camera Obscura & Outlook Tower Visitor Centre Castle Hill 031-226 3709. Open daily Oct–Mar 10–5; Apr–Sep 9.30–5.30. £1.45 (ch & pen 70p, students £1.10)

Candle Carvery and Museum Shop 140 High St 031-225 9566. Open daily 10–5.30. Free

Canongate Church Canongate, Royal Mile

Canongate Tolbooth 163 Canongate, Royal Mile 031-225 2424 ext 6638. Open Jun–Sep 10–6; Oct–May 10–5. Free

City Art Centre 2 Market St 031-225 2424 ext 6650 or 031-225 1131 after 5pm and weekends. Open Mon–Sat 10–5 (10–6 Jun–Sep) & Sun 2–5 during Edinburgh Festival. Free

City Chambers High St 031-225 2424. Open when Council business permits weekdays 10–3. Free

Craigmillar Castle (AM) Craigmillar. Open Apr–Sep Mon–Sat 9.30–7, Sun 2–7; Oct–Mar Mon–Sat 9.30–4, Sun 2–4 (closed Thu & Fri in winter). 50p (ch & pen 25p)

Edinburgh Castle (AM). Open 4 Jan–31 Mar & Oct–Dec Mon–Sat 9.30–4.20, Sun

82 DIRECTORY

12.30–3.35; Apr–Sep Mon–Sat 9.30–5.15, Sun 10.30–4.45. Castle closes 45 mins after the above times. £2 (ch & pen £1) Family £4.

Scottish National War Memorial Free. Also **Scottish United Services Museum** 031-225 7534. Open Mon–Sat 9.30–12.30 & 2–5, Sun 12.30–4.30. Free

Edinburgh Wax Museum 142 High St, Royal Mile 031-226 4445. Open daily 10–5 (last admission 4.30). £2.25 (ch 80p, pen 70p)

Edinburgh Zoo Corstorphine Rd 031-334 9171. Open all year Mon–Sat 9–6, Sun 9.30–6 (closes 5pm or dusk in winter). £2.50 (ch, pen & unemployed £1.25)

The Fruit Market Gallery 29 Market St 031-225 2383. Open Tue–Sat 10–5.30. Free

General Register House (east end of Princes St) 031-556 6585. Open all year Mon–Fri 9–4.45 Closed certain PH. Free

George Heriot's School Lauriston Place 031-229 7263. Open Jul–Aug Mon–Fri 9.30–4.30, Sat 9.30–11. Free

Georgian House (NTS) 7 Charlotte Square 031-225 2160. Open Apr–Oct Mon–Sat 10–5, Sun 2–5; Nov, Sat 10–4.30, Sun 2–4.30 (last admission ½hr before closing). £1.50 (ch 75p) (includes audio-visual shows)

Gladstone's Land (NTS) 483 Lawnmarket, High St 031-226 5856. Days and times of opening as Georgian House. £1.50 (ch 75p)

Greyfriars Bobby Candlemaker Row

Greyfriars Tolbooth & Highland Kirk Kirk of the Greyfriars, George IV Bridge

Heart of Midlothian near the west door of St Giles Cathedral

Huntly House 142 Canongate 031-225 2424 ext 6689 or 031-225 1131 after 5pm and weekends. Open Mon–Sat, Jun–Sep 10–6; Oct–May 10–5 (Sun 2–5 during Edinburgh Festival). Free

John Knox House Museum 45 High St 031-556 6961. Open Mon–Sat 10–5; Nov–Mar 10–4. Last admission 4.30pm, winter 3pm. £1 (ch & pen 70p)

Lady Stair's House off Lawnmarket 031-225 2424 ext 6593 (031-225 1131 after 5pm & weekends). Open Mon–Sat, Jun–Sep 10–6; Oct–May 10–5 (Sun 2–5 during Edinburgh Festival). Free

Lauriston Castle 2 Cramond Rd South, Davidson's Mains (on NW outskirts of Edinburgh, 1m E of Cramond) 031-336 2060. Open for guided tours only, Apr–Oct daily (ex Fri) 11–1 & 2–5 (last tour approx 4.20); Nov–Mar Sat & Sun only 2–4 (last tour approx 3.20). 80p (ch & pen 40p)

Magdalen Chapel Cowgate. For access contact Rev Sinclair Horne, Scottish Reformation Society, 17 George IV Bridge 031-225 1836

Museum of Childhood 42 High St, Royal Mile 031-225 2424 ext 6646. Open Mon–Sat 10–6 (Oct–May 10–5) (Sun 2–5 during Edinburgh Festival). Free

National Gallery of Scotland The Mound 031-556 8921. Open Mon–Sat 10–5, Sun 2–5; winter lunchtime closure (Oct–Mar) 12–1 West Gallery, 1–2 East Gallery and New Wing (Mon–Sat 10–6, Sun 11–6 during Edinburgh Festival). Free

National Library of Scotland George IV Bridge 031-226 4531. Reading rooms open Mon–Fri 9.30–8.30, Sat 9.30–1. Exhibition Mon–Fri 9.30–5, Sat 9.30–1. Sun (Apr–Sep only) 2–5. Free. Map Room Annexe 137 Causewayside. Open Mon–Fri 9.30–5, Sat 9.30–1. Free

Nelson Monument Calton Hill Open Apr–Sep Mon 1–6, Tue–Sat 10–6; Oct–Mar Mon–Sat 10–3. 45p

New Town Conservation Centre 13a Dundas St 031-556 7054. Open Mon–Fri 9–1 & 2–5. Free

Old St Paul's Church Carruber's Close

Palace of Holyroodhouse (at E end of Canongate) 031-556 7371. Open Mon–Sat 9.30–3.45. Guided tour of State and Historic Apartments. £1.50 (ch, pen & students 70p)

Parliament House with **Law Courts** Parliament Square (E of George IV Bridge) 031-225 2595. Open Mon–Fri 9.30–4. Free

Post Office Philatelic Bureau Waterloo Place 031-556 8661. Open Oct–Apr Mon–Fri 9–4.45, Sat 10–12.30; May–Sep Sat 10–12.30. Free

Royal Botanic Garden Inverleith Row 031-552 7171 ext 260. Garden open all year. Mar–Oct Mon–Sat 9–1hr before sunset, Sun 11–1hr before sunset; Oct–Mar Mon–Sat 9–sunset, Sun 11–sunset. Plant houses & exhibition hall open Mon–Sat 10–5, Sun 11–5 (from 10am during Edinburgh Festival). Free

Royal Museum of Scotland 9 Chambers St 031-225 7534. Open Mon–Sat 10–5, Sun 2–5. Free

Royal Museum of Scotland 1 Queen St 031-225 7534. Open Mon–Sat 10–5, Sun 2–5. Free

Royal Observatory Visitor Centre Blackford Hill 031-667 3321. Open Mon–Fri 10–4, Sat & Sun 12–5. 65p (ch & pen 35p)

Royal Scottish Academy The Mound 031-225 6671. Open Mon–Sat 10–5, Sun 2–5. £1.20 (ch & pen 50p)

St Giles Cathedral High St

St Mary's Episcopal Cathedral Palmerston Place

St Mary's Roman Catholic Cathedral Broughton St

Scott Monument East Princes Street Gardens. Open Apr–Sep Mon–Sat 9–6; Oct–Mar Mon–Sat 9–3. 45p

Scottish Craft Centre 140 Canongate, Royal Mile. Open Mon–Sat 10–5.30. Free

Scottish National Gallery of Modern Art Belford Rd 031-556 8921 ext 32. Open all year Mon–Sat 10–5, Sun 2–5

(Mon–Sat 10–6, Sun 11–6 during Edinburgh Festival). Free

Scottish National Portrait Gallery 1 Queen St 031-556 8921. Open Mon–Sat 10–5, Sun 2–5 (Mon–Sat 10–6, Sun 11–6 during Edinburgh Festival). Free

Talbot Rice Art Centre 031-667 1011 ext 4308. Open all year Mon–Fri 10–5, Sat 10–1. Free

Tron Church Hunter Square

West Register House Charlotte Square 031-556 6585. Open Mon–Fri, 9–4.45 (ex PH). Free

AROUND EDINBURGH

Aberdour Castle (AM) Open Apr–Sep Mon–Sat 9.30–7, Sun 2–7; Oct–Mar Mon–Sat 9.30–4, Sun 2–4. Closed Thu am & Fri in winter. Admission fee payable

Andrew Carnegie Birthplace Museum Moodie St Dunfermline (0383) 724302. Open all year daily. Apr–Oct Mon–Sat 11–5 (Wed 8pm), Sun 2–5; Nov–Mar 2–4 daily. Free

Blackness Castle (AM) 4½m NE of Linlithgow. Open Apr–Sep Mon–Sat 9.30–7, Sun 2–7; Oct–Mar Mon–Sat 9.30–4, Sun 2–4. Closed Mon pm & Tue in winter. Admission fee payable

Bo'ness and Kinneil Railway off Union St (0506) 822298. Trains run Etr, 6 May, 27 May & 26 Aug and weekends until end Sep

Bowhill Selkirk (2½m off A708) (0750) 20732. Grounds open May–Aug 12–5, riding centre all year. House & grounds 4 Jul–16 Aug Mon–Sat (closed Fri) 1–4.30, Sun 2–6. House & grounds £2, grounds only 80p

Castle Campbell (AM) and **Dollar Glen (NTS)** Dollar (1m N) *Glen* Open 4 Jan–23 Mar & 1 Oct–31 Dec Mon–Sat 9.30–4.20, Sun 12.30–3.35; 24 Mar–30 Sep Mon–Sat 9.30–5.05, Sun 11–5.05. Closed Thu pm & Fri in winter
Castle Open Apr–Sep Mon–Sat 9.30–7, Sun 2–7; Oct–Mar Mon–Sat 9.30–4, Sun 2–4. (Closed Thu pm & Fri in winter.) Admission fee payable

Castle Jail Castlegate, Jedburgh (0835) 63254. Open Etr–mid Sep Mon–Sat 10–12 & 1–5, Sun 2–5. 50p (ch 16, students, pen & unemployed 35p)

Crichton Castle (AM) Crichton. Open Apr–Sep Mon–Sat 9.30–7, Sun 2–7; Oct–Mar weekends only 2–4. Admission fee payable

Culross Abbey (AM) Culross. Open Apr–Sep Mon–Sat 9.30–7, Sun 2–7; Oct–Mar Mon–Sat 9.30–4, Sun 2–4. Free

Culross Palace (AM) Culross. Open Apr–Sep Mon–Sat 9.30–7, Sun 2–7; Oct–Mar Mon–Sat 9.30–4, Sun 2–4. Admission fee payable

Dalkeith Park Buccleuch Estate, Dalkeith 031-663 5684. Open end Mar–Oct daily 11–6, Nov weekends only. 65p

Dalmeny House South Queensferry 031-331 1888. Open 3 May–30 Sep, Sun–Thu 2–5.30 (last admission 5pm). £1.80 (ch 5–16 & students £1.20, pen £1.50)

Dawyck Botanic Garden on B712, 8m SW of Peebles (07216) 254. Open Apr–Sep daily 9–5. 50p per car

Dirleton Castle (AM) Dirleton. Open Apr–Sep Mon–Sat 9.30–4, Sun 2–7; Oct–Mar Mon–Sat 9.30–4, Sun 2–4. £1 (ch & pen 50p)

Dryburgh Abbey (AM) Open Apr–Sep Mon–Sat 9.30–7, Sun 2–7; Oct–Mar Mon–Sat 9.30–4, Sun 2–4. Admission fee payable

Dunfermline Abbey (AM) Pittencrieff Park, Dunfermline. Open Apr–Sep Mon–Sat 9.30–7, Sun 2–7; Oct–Mar Mon–Sat 9.30–4, Sun 2–4. Free

Earlshall Castle Leuchars (033483) 205. Open Etr–27 Sep Thu–Sun 2–6 (last admission 5.15pm). £2 (ch 5–16 £1, pen £1.50)

Edinburgh Butterfly Farm Melville Nurseries, Lasswade 031-663 4932. Open Apr–Oct daily 10–6, (10–5.30 Sat & Sun). £1.75 (ch & pen £1).

DIRECTORY 83

Family Ticket, 2 adults and up to 4 children, £5

Edinburgh Crystal Visitors Centre Eastfield, Penicuik (10m S of Edinburgh) (0968) 75128. Open Mon–Sat 9–5, and some Sun. Tours Mon–Fri 9–3.30

Falkland Palace & Garden (NTS) Falkland (0337) 57397. Palace and Garden open Apr–Sep Mon–Sat 10–6, Sun 2–6; Oct Sat 10–6, Sun 2–6. Last visitors to Palace 5.15. Palace and Gardens £1.80 (ch 16 90p). Garden only £1.20 (ch 16 60p)

Fife Folk Museum The Weigh House, Ceres (033482) 380 (curator's house). Open Apr–Oct, Mon, Wed–Sat 2–5, Sun 2.30–5.30. Admission fee payable

Floors Castle Kelso (0573) 23333. Castle open Etr Sun & Mon, then 3 May–30 Sep Sun–Thu. Also open Fri in Jul & Aug 10.30–5.30 (last admission to Castle 4.45pm). Walled garden and garden centre, daily 9.30–5. £2 (ch 8 & over £1.30, pen £1.60). Grounds £1.20

Gladstone Court Museum entrance by 113 High St, Biggar (0899) 21050. Open Etr–Oct daily 10–12.30, 2–5; Sun 2–5. Admission fee payable

Greenhill Covenanters House Burn Braes, Biggar (0899) 21050. Open Etr–mid Oct daily 2–5. Admission fee payable

Hailes Castle (AM) East Linton (1m SW on unclassified road). Open Apr–Sep Mon–Sat 9.30–7, Sun 2–7; Oct–Mar Mon–Sat 9.30–4, Sun 2–4 (closed Wed pm and Thu in winter). Admission fee payable

Hill of Tarvit Mansion House & Garden (NTS) (2m S of Cupar off A916) (0334) 53127. Open Etr weekend, Apr & Oct Sat & Sun 2–6; May–Sep daily 2–6. Last admission ½hr before closing. Garden and grounds open all year 9.30–sunset. House & Garden £1.80 (ch 90p). Garden only 60p (ch 30p)

The Hirsel Coldstream (½m W on A697) (0890) 2834. Open

during daylight hours. Admission by donation

Hopetoun House South Queensferry (2m W on unclassified road) 031-331 2451. Open Etr then May–mid Sep daily 11–5. Admission fee payable

House of the Binns (NTS) (4m E of Linlithgow off A904). Open Etr then May–Sep daily (ex Fri) 2–5, last admission 4.30pm. Parkland daily 10–sunset. £1.80 (ch 90p). Members of the Royal Scots Dragoon Guards free when in uniform

Jane Welsh Carlyle Museum Lodge St, Haddington (062082) 3738. Open Apr–Sep Wed–Sat 2–5. 50p (accompanied ch free, pen 30p)

Jedburgh Abbey (AM) Open Apr–Sep Mon–Sat 9.30–7, Sun 2–7; Oct–Mar Mon–Sat 9.30–4, Sun 2–4. Closed Thu pm & Fri in winter. £1 (ch & pen 50p)

Kailzie Gardens (2½m SE of Peebles on B7062) (0721) 20007. Open 4 Apr–11 Oct daily 11–5.30. £1 (ch 35p)

Kellie Castle & Gardens (NTS) (2m N of St Monans off B9171) (03338) 271. Castle open Etr & Oct Sat & Sun 2–6; May–Sep daily 2–6. Garden & grounds all year daily 10–sunset. Castle & gardens £1.80 (ch 90p). Gardens only 80p (accompanied ch 40p)

Kelso Abbey (AM) Open Apr–Sep Mon–Sat 9.30–7, Sun 2–7; Oct–Mar Mon–Sat 9.30–4, Sun 2–4. Free

Kinneil House (AM) Bo'ness Open Apr–Sep Mon–Sat 9.30–7, Sun 2–7; Oct–Mar Mon–Sat 9.30–4, Sun 2–4 (Closed Tue pm & Fri in winter). 50p (ch & pen 25p)

Linlithgow Palace (AM) Linlithgow. Open Apr–Sep Mon–Sat 9.30–7, Sun 2–7; Oct–Mar Mon–Sat 9.30–4, Sun 2–4. £1 (ch & pen 50p)

Loch Leven Castle (AM) Castle Island, Kinross. Open Apr–Sep 9.30–7 (Sun 2–7) 50p (ch & pen 25p). Ferry charge

Malleny Garden (NTS) off Bavelaw Rd, Balerno. Open May–Sep daily 10–sunset £1 (ch 50p). Charge box

Manderston (1¼m E of Duns off A6105) (0361) 83450. Open 14 May–27 Sep, Sun & Thu 2–5.30. Also open BH. Admission fee payable

Mary, Queen of Scots House Queen Street, Jedburgh (0835) 63331. Open Etr–Oct Mon–Sat 10–12 & 1–5, Sun 1–5 (& 10–12, Jun–Oct only). £1 (ch 16, unemployed, students & pen 75p)

Mellerstain House (3m S of Gordon on unclassified road) (057381) 225. Open Etr, then May–Sep Mon–Fri & Sun 12.30–5. (Last admission 4.30pm.) Admission fee payable

Melrose Abbey (AM) Melrose. Open Apr–Sep Mon–Sat 9.30–7, Sun 2–7; Oct–Mar Mon–Sat 9.30–4, Sun 2–4. £1 (ch & pen 50p)

Melrose Motor Museum Newstead Rd, Melrose (0835) 22356. Open Apr–Oct, daily 10.30–5.30, Nov–Mar Sat & Sun 10–5. Admission fee payable

Museum of Flight East Fortune Airport, East Fortune 031-225 7534. Open Jul & Aug Mon–Sat 10–5, Sun 11–5, also Open Days. Free

Myreton Motor Museum Aberlady (08757) 288. Open daily 10–6 (10–5 in winter). £1 (ch 16 25p)

Neidpath Castle Peebles (08757) 201. Open 16 Apr–Oct, Mon–Sat 10–1 & 2–6, Sun 1–6, subject to the availability of staff. 75p (ch 14 20p, ch under 4 free, pen 50p)

Nether Mill (Peter Anderson Ltd) Huddersfield St, Galashiels (0896) 2091. Open Apr–Oct Mon–Sat 9–5, (Jun–Sep Sun 12–5); Mill tours Mon–Fri between 10.30 and 2. Free

Pinkie House Musselburgh 031-665 2059. Open mid Apr–mid Jul & mid Sep–mid Dec, Tue 2–5. Free

Preston Mill (NTS) East Linton (0620) 860426. Open Apr–Sep Mon–Sat 10–12.30 & 2–5.30, Sun 2–5.30; Oct Mon–Sat 10–12.30 & 2–4.30, Sun 2–4.30; Nov–Mar Sat 10–12.30 & 2–4.30, Sun 2–4.30. £1 (ch 16 50p)

Priorwood Garden (NTS) Melrose (089682) 2965. Open Apr & 1 Nov–24 Dec, Mon–Sat 10–1 & 2–5.30; May–Jun & Oct Mon–Sat 10–5.30, Sun 1.30–5.30; Jul–Sep Mon–Sat 10–6, Sun 1.30–5.30. Donations

St Andrews Castle (AM) St Andrews. Open Apr–Sep Mon–Sat 9.30–7, Sun 2–7; Oct–Mar Mon–Sat 9.30–4, Sun 2–4. Admission fee payable

St Andrews Cathedral & Museum (AM) St Andrews. Open Apr–Sep Mon–Sat 9.30–7, Sun 2–7; Oct–Mar Mon–Sat 9.30–4, Sun 2–4. 50p (ch 25p)

Scottish Agricultural Museum Royal Highland Showground, Ingliston 031-225 7534. Open May–Sep Mon–Fri 10–5, Sun 11–5. Free

Scottish Fisheries Museum St Ayles, Harbour Head, Anstruther (0333) 310628. Open Nov–Mar daily (ex Tue) 2–5; Apr–Oct Mon–Sat 10–5.30, Sun 2–5. £1 (ch 16, pen & unemployed 50p)

Scottish Mining Museum Lady Victoria Colliery, Newtongrange 031-663 7519. Open Tue–Fri 10–4.30, Sat & Sun 12–5. Admission fee payable

Scottish Museum of Woollen Textiles Tweedvale Mill, Walkerburn (089687) 281 & 283. Open Etr–Oct Mon–Sat 10–5, Sun 12–4.30; winter Mon–Fri 10–5. Admission fee payable

Smailholm Tower (AM) (1½m SW of Smailholm). Open Apr–Sep Mon–Sat 9.30–7, Sun 2–7; Oct–Mar Mon–Sat 9.30–4, Sun 2–4. 50p (ch 25p)

Tantallon Castle (AM) (2m E of North Berwick on A198). Open Apr–Sep Mon–Sat 9.30–7, Sun 2–7; Oct–Mar Mon–Sat 9.30–4, Sun 2–4. (Closed Tue & alternate Wed in winter). £1 (ch & pen 50p)

Thirlestane Castle & Border Country Life Museum Lauder (05782) 254. Open Etr, May, Jun & Sep, Wed, Thu & Sun;

Jul & Aug daily ex Sat. Castle & Museum 2–5; Grounds 12–6. £2 (ch & pen £1.50). Family £5

Torphichen Preceptory (AM) Open Apr–Sep Mon–Sat 9.30–7, Sun 2–7; Oct–Mar Mon–Sat 9.30–4, Sun 2–4, closed Fri & alternate Wed. Closed in winter. 50p (ch & pen 25p)

Town House & The Study (NTS) Culross (0383) 880359. Open: House Etr & May–Sep Mon–Fri 10–1 & 2–5, Sat & Sun 2–5; Study Apr–Oct Sat & Sun 2–4 also by appointment. House 50p (ch & pen 25p). Study 30p (ch & pen 15p)

Traquair House Traquair (1m S of Innerleithen on B709) (0896) 830323. Open 12 Apr–18 Oct 1.30–5.30. Jul, Aug & first 2 weeks in Sep open 10.30–5.30. Last admission 5pm. House admission fee payable

Tynighame Gardens Dunbar (1m N of A1 between Dunbar & East Linton) (0620) 860330. Open Jun–Sep Mon–Fri 10.30–4.30. Admission fee payable

Entertainment

THEATRES AND CONCERT HALLS

Assembly Rooms 54 George St 031-226 5992. International lunchtime concerts

Church Hill Theatre Morningside Rd 031-447 7597

King's Theatre Leven St 031-229 1201. Scottish Opera, musicals, pantomimes

The Netherbow Arts Centre 43 High St 031-556 9579

The Playhouse Theatre 22 Greenside Pl 031-557 2590. Scottish Ballet; rock concerts; grand opera

The Queen's Hall Clerk St 031-668 3456. Home of the Scottish Chamber Orchestra and the Scottish Baroque Ensemble; also jazz and pop concerts, folk music, recitals

Royal Lyceum Theatre Grindlay St 031-229 9697

The Scottish Youth Theatre 48 Albany St 031-557 0962

Theatre Workshop 34 Hamilton Place 031-226 5425

Traverse Theatre 112 West Bow, Grassmarket 031-226 2633. New work by contemporary Scottish and international writers

Usher Hall Lothian Rd 031-228 1155. Scottish Chamber Orchestra; Scottish National Orchestra

CINEMAS

Cameo Cinema Tollcross 031-228 4141

Cannon 1, 2 & 3 120 Lothian Rd 031-229 3030

Classic Cinema 50 Nicolson St 031-667 1839

Dominion Cinemas Newbattle Terrace 031-447 2660

Filmhouse 88 Lothian Rd 031-228 2688

Odeon Theatre Clerk St 031-667 7331/2

DISCOS/NIGHTCLUBS

Amphitheatre Lothian Rd 031-229 7670. Most modern lightshow in Scotland

Buster Browns 25 Market St 031-226 4224. Open Thu–Sun 9.30pm–3am

Cinderellas Rockerfellers St Stephen St 031-556 0266. Open Tue–Sun

Coasters Discotheque Complex 3 West Tollcross 031-228 3252. Open Fri–Sun

Dillingers 28 King's Stables Rd 031-228 3547. Open Thu–Sun

Madhatters 126 High St 031-225 4343. Open Fri 9pm–3am; Sat 10pm–3am

Madisons Greenside Place (next to Playhouse Theatre) 031-557 3807. Open Thu, Fri & Sat (Sun from March onwards), 21+ 9.30pm–3am

Top 'O' Nightspot 40 Grindlay St 031-229 6697. Open daily 10pm–3am

Zenatec 3 Semple St 031-229 7733 (night), 031-229 8522 (day). Open Fri, Sat & Sun

CASINOS

The Berkeley Casino Club 2 Rutland Place 031-228 4446. Open Mon–Fri 2pm–4am, Sat 2pm–2am, Sun 7.30pm–4am (membership takes 48hrs to process)

Casino Martell 7 Newington Rd 031-667 7763. Open Mon–Fri 10pm–4am; Sat 10pm–2am; Sun 10pm–4am

Royal Chimes Casino 3 Royal Terrace 031-556 1055. Open Mon–Fri 2pm–4am; Sat 7pm–2am; Sun 9pm–4am

Stakis Regency Casino 14 Picardy Place 031-557 3585. Open Mon–Fri 2pm–4am; Sat 2pm–2am; Sun 7.30pm–4am (membership takes 48hrs to process)

EVENING/LUNCHTIME ENTERTAINMENT

Bannermans Bar 212 Cowgate 031-556 3254. Jazz, blues & folk music

Platform One Caledonian Hotel, Rutland St 031-225 2433. Jazz, blues & folk music

Crest Hotel Queensferry Rd 031-332 2442. Jazz

SCOTTISH EVENINGS

The hotels listed below offer visitors to Edinburgh an enjoyable evening of traditional Scottish food and entertainment.

George Hotel George St 031-225 1251

King James Thistle Hotel Leith St 031-556 0111

Learmonth Hotel 18–20 Learmonth Terrace 031-343 2671. Entertainment available only

North British Hotel Princes St 031-556 2414

Round Stables Prestonfield House Hotel, Prestonfield Rd, Prestonfield 031-668 3346

DIRECTORY

Recreation and Sport

BOWLING GREENS

Balgreen
Canaan Grove
St Margarets Park, Corstorphine
Dalmeny Street
Harrison
Inverleith Park
Jessfield
Leith Links
Loaning Crescent
The Meadows (East and West)
Montgomery Street
Oxgangs
Powderhall
Prestonfield
Stenhouse
Victoria Park

FISHING

RESERVOIRS AND LOCHS

These are located near Edinburgh and are mainly stocked with brown and/or rainbow trout.

Bonaly Reservoir (no permit required)
Clubbiedean Reservoir
Crosswood Reservoir
Gladhouse Reservoir
Glencourse Reservoir
Harlaw Reservoir
Harperrig Reservoir
Permits for the above are available from Lothian Regional Council, Department of Water and Drainage, Comiston Springs, Buckstone Terrace, Edinburgh 031-445 4141.

Donolly Reservoir
Hopes Reservoir
Permits available from Lothian Regional Council, Department of Water and Drainage, Alderston House, Haddington (062 082) 4131

Duddingston Loch (carp, perch, roach, tench). Permits from Scottish Development Dept, 3–11 Melville St, Edinburgh 031-226 2570

RIVERS

River Esk Permits from T Mealyou, Sports Shop, 11 Newbiggin, Musselburgh

River Esk (North) Permits from Esk Valley Angling Improvement Association, Kevin Burns, 53 Fernieside Crescent, Edinburgh 031-664 4685 or local shops. Officials on river

Water of Leith Permits from Lothian Regional Council Reception, George IV Bridge, Edinburgh

River Tyne Permits from J S Main (Saddlers), 87 High St, Haddington

Union Canal Permits from Ranger, Union Canal Lothian Regional Council, George IV Bridge, Edinburgh.

SEA AND SHORE

There is sea and shore angling at South Queensferry and Musselburgh. In Edinburgh there is shore angling at Cramond, the mouth of the River Almond, and from Seafield to Portobello.

FOOTBALL

Heart of Midlothian Football Club Tynecastle Park 031-337 6132

Hibernian Football Club Easter Road Park 031-661 2159

GOLF COURSES

Visitors are generally welcome at the golf clubs listed below. Some clubs do impose certain restrictions and where this is the case these have been noted at the end of each entry. It is advisable to telephone in advance and check when starting times are available. Clubs and trolleys are available for hire at many clubs. For more details on golf courses, please see the current edition of *AA Guide to Golf Courses in Britain*.

NEAR CITY CENTRE (within 5-mile radius)

Braid Hills Golf Courses (2 municipal courses) Braid Hills Approach 031-447 6666. 2½ miles from the city centre off the A702

The Bruntsfield Links Golfing Society Ltd 32 Barnton Ave 031-336 1479 4 miles north-west of the city off the A90 to Queensferry. Members of recognised golf clubs require a letter of introduction

Carrick Knowe Golf Course (municipal course) off Balgreen Rd 031-337 1096. 2 miles west of the city centre, off the A8. Near Murrayfield Rugby Ground

Craigentinny Golf Course (municipal course) Craigentinny Ave 031-554 7501. 2½ miles east of the city centre off A199 Seafield Road

Craigmillar Park Golf Club 1 Observatory Rd 031-667 0047. 2½ miles south of city centre off A701. Terms for visitors available from the Secretary

Duddingston Golf Club Duddingston Rd West 031-661 7688 (Secretary). 3 miles east of city centre on the A1

Gogarburn Hospital Golf Club Gogarburn Hospital 031-339 4242. Off the main Edinburgh/Glasgow road, west of the Maybury roundabout

Kingsknowe Golf Club 326 Lanark Rd 031-441 1145. 3 miles south-west from city centre on A70. Restrictions on visitors at weekends

Liberton Golf Club Kingston Grange, 297 Gilmerton Rd 031-664 3009. 2½ miles south-east of the city centre off the A68

Lothianburn Golf Club Biggar Rd 031-445 2288. 5 miles south of the city centre on the A702. Restricted times for visitors at weekends

Mortonhall Golf Club 231 Braid Rd 031-447 2411. 4 miles south of city centre, on Braid Road off A702. Visitors require a letter of introduction from their home club

Murrayfield Golf Club 43 Murrayfield Rd 031-337 3478. 2 miles west of city centre off the A8. Visitors require a letter of introduction from their home club and must book in advance by telephone. Weekdays only.

DIRECTORY 87

Portobello Golf Course (municipal course) Stanley St 031-669 4361. 3 miles east of the city centre off the A1

Prestonfield Golf Club Prestonfield Rd North 031-667 1273. 1½ miles south-east of city centre off the A68. Members of recognised golf clubs welcome. Some weekend restrictions

Ravelston Golf Club 24 Ravelston Dykes Rd 031-332 3486. 2½ miles west of city centre between the A90 and the A8. Visitors (from outside Scotland) welcome weekdays

The Royal Burgess Golfing Society Whitehouse Rd, Barton 031-339 2075 (Secretary). 4 miles north-west of city centre off the A90. Visitors welcome weekdays on application to the Secretary

Silverknowes Golf Course (municipal) Silverknowes Parkway 031-336 3843. 4 miles north-west of the city centre off the A90

Swanston Golf Club Swanston Rd 031-445 2239. 5 miles south of city centre off A702

Torphin Hill Golf Club Torphin Rd, Colinton 031-441 1100. 3 miles south-west of city centre off A720

Turnhouse Golf Club 154 Turnhouse Rd, Corstorphine 031-339 7701. 5 miles out of city, near Edinburgh Airport

Port Royal Golf Range Eastfield Rd (next to Edinburgh Airport) 031-335 4377. Open daily. Floodlit bays; practice sand bunkers; putting green; professional tuition

FURTHER AFIELD

Blairgowrie Golf Club Rosemount, Blairgowrie (0250) 2622. 1½ miles south of Blairgowrie on the A93. Starting times to be booked in advance in writing. Some restrictions Wednesdays and weekends

Dalmahoy Country Club Kirknewton 031-333 1845. 7½ miles west of Edinburgh on the A71

Gleneagles Hotel Golf Courses Auchterarder (07646) 3543. 2 miles west of Auchterarder on A823

Gullane Golf Club Gullane (0620) 843115. 21 miles north-east of Edinburgh on the A198. Some restrictions on No 1 course

The Honourable Company of Edinburgh Golfers Muirfield, Gullane (0620) 842123. 18 miles east of Edinburgh on the A198. Visitors are requested to must make prior application through home golf club secretary

Ladybank Golf Club Ladybank (0337) 30320. 6 miles south of Cupar

The Links Golf Course Musselburgh. On the A1 next to Musselburgh Racecourse

Longniddry Golf Club Longniddry (0875) 52141. 13 miles east of Edinburgh. No visitors Fridays and weekends

Lundin Golf Club Golf Rd, Lundin Links (0333) 320202. 13 miles east of Kirkcaldy on A915

The Musselburgh Golf Club Monktonhall, Musselburgh 031-665 2005. East of Edinburgh off the A1. Visitors must book in advance in writing

North Berwick Golf Club The Clubhouse, West Links, North Berwick (0620) 2666. North-east of Edinburgh off the A198

Ratho Park Golf Club Ratho, Newbridge 031-333 1752. 8 miles west of Edinburgh

Royal Musselburgh Golf Club Prestongrange House, Prestonpans (0875) 276. 9 miles east of Edinburgh on the A198

St Andrews Links Management Committee, Golf Place, St Andrews (4 public courses). Tel (0334) 75757 to make advance bookings

GREYHOUND RACING

Powderhall Stadium Beaverhall Rd 031-556 8141. Also athletics

HORSE RACING

Musselburgh Racecourse 031-665 2859

ICE SPORTS

Murrayfield Ice Rink Riversdale Crescent 031-337 6933. Skating, ice hockey

MOTOR RACING

Royal Highland Showground Ingliston road-racing circuit. Meetings held Apr–Oct

PONY TREKKING AND RIDING

Grange Riding Centre Mrs E Knight, West Calder (0506) 871219

Silverknowes Riding Centre Muirhouse Parkway 031-332 5750

Tower Farm Riding Stables Mrs J Forrest, 85 Liberton Drive 031-664 3375

PUTTING

Bruntsfield
St Margarets Park, Corstorphine
Harrison
Inverleith
Leith Links
Pilrig Park
Portobello (Novelty golf)
East Princes Street Gardens
Rosefield
Saughton
Victoria Park

PITCH AND PUTT

Bruntsfield Park 18 holes

Inverleith Park Apr–Sep, 9 holes

RUGBY

Murrayfield Scottish Rugby Union Ground Roseburn St 031-337 8993

SKIING

Hillend Ski Centre Biggar Rd, Pentland Hills 031-445 4433. 400-metre artificial ski slope

SNOOKER

Angle Club 3 Jordan Lane 031-447 8700

Cuemasters Snooker and Social Club 183 Constitution St 031-554 0971

Davis Snooker Club 24 Annandale St 031-557 4579

Marco's Leisure Centre 51–95 Grove Street 031-228 2141

DIRECTORY

Snooker and Squash Centre
146 Slateford Rd 031-443 2211

SPORTS CENTRES

Craiglockhart Sports Centre
177 Colinton Rd 031-443 0101/2

Jack Kane Centre 208 Niddrie Main Rd 031-669 0404

Meadowbank Sports Centre
139 London Rd 031-661 5351

Saughton Sports Centre 031-443 0101/2

SWIMMING

Telephone enquiries for all the swimming centres listed below should be directed to the Royal Commonwealth Pool 031-667 7211

Dalry Teaching Centre Caledonian Crescent. Open Mon–Fri, 12 noon–1.20; Tue, Thu & Fri 5.30–8; Sat 9–4; Sun 9–12noon

Glenogle Swimming Centre Glenogle Rd. Open Mon–Fri 12noon–8; Sat 9–4; Sun 9–12noon

Infirmary Street Swimming Centre Infirmary St. Open Mon–Fri 8–8; Sat 9–4

Leith Swimming Centre Junction Pl, Leith. Open Mon–Fri 9–8; Sat 9–4

Portobello Swimming Centre Bellfield St. Open Mon–Fri 9–8; Sat 9–6

Royal Commonwealth Pool 21 Dalkeith Rd. Open Mon–Fri 9–9; Sat & Sun 10–4 (swimming, diving, sauna/solarium suite, fitness centre, rowing tank, pool tables etc)

Shopping

There are pedestrian shopping precincts at Rose Street (between Princes Street and George Street), in the St James' Centre and the Waverley Market. Most of the larger shops and department stores (British Home Stores, C & A, Frasers, Jenners, Littlewoods, Marks & Spencer) are situated in Princes Street.

ANTIQUE SHOPS

Alexander Adamson 48 St Stephen St 031-225 7310. General antiques, Georgian furniture, porcelain, glass

Aldric Young 49 Thistle St 031-226 4101. Late 18th- and early 19th-century antiques

Joseph Bonnar 72 Thistle St 031-226 2811. Antique and period jewellery, small silver

Carson Clark Gallery (Scotia Maps) 173 Canongate 031-556 4710. Antique maps

Castle Antiques
330 Lawnmarket 031-225 7615. Furniture, china, pictures, silver

Cavanagh (The Collector's Shop) 49 Cockburn St 031-226 3391. Coins, medals, postcards, cigarette cards, jewellery, antique silver, militaria

Court Curio Shop
519 Lawnmarket 031-225 3972. Jewellery, general

Paul Couts 101 West Bow 031-225 3238. 18th-century furniture

Eric Davidson 4 Grassmarket 031-225 5815. Furniture, porcelain, silverware, paintings

Dunedin Antiques 4 North West Circus Pl 031-226 3074. Furniture, metalwork

Tom Fidelo 49 Cumberland St 031-557 2444. Antique paintings

Fifteen Grassmarket
15 Grassmarket 031-226 3087. Period clothes. Open Mon–Fri 1–7pm, all day Sat

Fyfes Antiques 41 & 48 Thistle St 031-225 4287. Furniture, porcelain, oil paintings

Goodwin 15 Queensferry St 031-225 4717. Silver jewellery

Herrald 38 Queen St 031-225 5939. Antique furniture, silver, brass

Humphrey 38 Victoria St 031-226 3625. Postcards, china, glass, paintings

Letham Antiques 20 Dundas St 031-556 6565. Furniture, silver, jewellery, decorative items. Closed Mon

Linton 95 West Bow 031-226 6946. Prints, paintings, bric-a-brac

John McIntosh 60 Grassmarket 031-225 1165. Fine art, porcelain, bric-a-brac

Penny Farthing 7 Beaufort Rd 031-447 2410. General

West Bow Antiques 102 West Bow 031-226 2852

John Whyte 116 Rose St 031-226 2377. Jewellery, silver (new and antique)

Whytock and Reid Sunbury House, Belford Mews 031-226 4911. 18th- and 19th-century British furniture, oriental carpets and rugs, church furnishings

Wildman Brothers
54 Hanover St 031-225 6754. Jewellery, china, silver

BOOKSHOPS

Automobile Association
18–22 Melville St

Bauermeister Booksellers 19 George IV Bridge

Edinburgh Bookshop 57 George St

Church of Scotland Bookshop 117 George St

James Thin 53 South Bridge

Waterstone's Booksellers 114 George St (off Charlotte Sq)

CRAFT SHOPS

Curio Imports 14 & 44 Leven St 031-229 0899. Oriental curios, crafts, clothes

Ian Clarkson 87 West Bow 031-225 8141. Contemporary British craft jewellery

Eastern Crafts 251/253 Canongate 031-556 6553. Oriental curios and crafts

Edinburgh Candles Shop
42 Candlemaker Row 031-225 9646. Candles, cards, incense

Innes Art 219 Bruntsfield Pl 031-447 8929. Art, jewellery

Langue de Chat Unit 8, Waverley Market 031-556 8100. Designer knitwear

Potters Choice 13 St Mary's St 031-556 6751. Pottery, crafts, giftwrap

Romulus 136 Rose St 031-226 5269. Glass, soft toys, pottery, gifts

Royal Mile Miniatures 154 Canongate 031-557 2293. Specialises in making furniture for dolls' houses

Sandpiper Crafts 106 Rose St 031-226 6211. Jewellery, gifts, giftwrap, crafts

Clare Schilska 46 Candlemaker Row 031-225 1191

Scotrocks 10 Grassmarket 031-226 6383

Scottish Craft Centre 140 Canongate 031-556 6051. Display of selected Scottish craft work for sale. Exhibitions, advisory service. Open Mon–Sat 10–5.30, admission free

Studio One 10–14 Stafford St 031-226 5812. Also furniture shop at 132 Morningside Rd

and kitchen shop at 71 Morningside Rd

Anne Thomas Fabrics 274 Canongate 031-557 1503

DELICATESSENS

The Good Food Shop 213 St John's Rd 031-334 2159

Henderson's 94 Hanover St 031-225 2131. Vegetarian, wholefood

Herby's Delicatessen 66 Raeburn Pl 031-332 9888

Nastiuk Continental Delicatessen 10 Gillespie Pl 031-229 7054. International food specialist

Newington Road Delicatessen 84 Newington Rd 031-667 2969. Wholefood, continental specialities, duck, quail, goose

Valvona & Crolla 19 Elm Row 031-556 6066. Continental food and wine

Victor Hugo Delicatessen 26–27 Melville Terr 031-667 1827. Continental meats, paté, farmhouse cheese, fish

DRY CLEANER

Pullars 23 Frederick St 031-

225 8095. Mon–Fri 8.30–5.30 Sat 8.30–1

TARTANS AND WOOLLENS

Discount Highland Supply 7 Cowgatehead

Edinburgh Woollen Mill 62 & 139 Princes St

Geoffrey (Tailor) Highland Crafts 57–59 High St

Gleneagles of Scotland 371 High St

The House of Macpherson 17 West Maitland St, Haymarket

The Kilt Shop 21–25 George IV Bridge

Kinloch Anderson Ltd John Knox House, 45 High St

Pitlochry Knitwear 28 North Bridge

Rodger of the Royal Mile 3 Canongate

The Scotch House 60 Princes St

Romanes & Paterson 62 Princes St

Scotia Kilt Shop 84 Causewayside

Tartan Gift Shop 96–96a Princes St

Transport

BUS SERVICES

For local bus and tour information contact:

Lothian Region Transport 5 Waverley Bridge 031-226 5087 and 031-554 4494 (lost property)

Eastern Scottish Buses St Andrew Square Bus Station 031-556 8464

Last buses to termini leave the city centre Mon–Sat at 11.30pm, Sun 11pm (times approx). There are five circular night bus services from Waverley Bridge which serve many parts of the city and immediate areas, Mon–Fri 0.15am, 1.15am, 2.15am, 3.15am and 4.15am; Sat & Sun 0.15am, 1.15am 2.15am and 3.15am.

A Freedom Ticket, available from Lothian Region Transport and the Tourist Information

Centre, allows unlimited use of the city buses for one day (not valid for the Airport Service).

An Airport Bus, service 100, operates between Edinburgh Airport and Waverley Bridge. Timetables are available from Lothian Region Transport, address as above.

CAR HIRE

When making enquiries, ask for a fully inclusive rate to include car hire, insurance, 15% VAT, any mileage charge and any other surcharges. Also check your liability in case of any damage to the vehicle as you may have to pay the first part of a claim even if you are insured.

Arnold Clark Lochrin, Tolcross 031-229 8911

Avis Rent A Car 100 Dalry Rd 031-337 6363

Avis Rent A Car Terminal Buiding, Edinburgh Airport 031-333 1866

Bradbury Vehicle Rentals 37–40 Haddington Pl 031-556 1406

Budget Rent A Car 116 Polwarth Gardens 031-228 6088

City Car Rental Coach Terminal, 14 Lothian Rd 031-228 3409

Edinburgh Car and Van Rental 9 Cranston St 031-556 1666

Forth Car Hire Learmonth Hotel, 19 Learmonth Terr 031-343 1001

Godfrey Davis Europcar 24 East London St 031-661 1252

Godfrey Davis Europcar Terminal Building, Edinburgh Airport 031-333 2588

DIRECTORY

Godfrey Davis Europcar Waverley Rail Drive Kiosk 031-556 8835

Hertz Rent A Car 10 Picardy Pl 031-556 8311

Mitchells Self Drive Car Hire 32 Torphichen St 031-229 5384

Roadrunner Car Hire 24 Haymarket Terr 031-337 1319

Total Car Rental 45 Lochrin Pl 031-229 4548

CAR PARKS

MULTI-STOREY CAR PARKS

St James Centre
Castle Terrace

SURFACE CAR PARKS

Crichton Street
Haymarket Terrace
Holyrood Road
Lauriston Place
Leith Street
Morrison Street
St Leonard's Street
West Nicolson Street

TAXIS

Castle Cars 2 Torphichen St 031-228 2555

Central Radio Taxis 163 Gilmore Pl 031-229 5221

City Cabs 2 Atholl Pl 031-228 1211

Handicabs (Lothian) Ltd 14 Braefoot Terr 031-666 0955

Radiocabs 5 Upper Bow 031-225 9000, 031-225 6736

BRITISH RAIL

The following list shows the approximate train journey times to destinations within Scotland:
Edinburgh—Glasgow
45 mins
Edinburgh—Inverness
4 hours
Edinburgh—Aberdeen
2½ hours

For the latest information on rail fares, destinations and enquiries about services, contact your local station or telephone:

British Rail Waverley Station 031-556 2451

Useful information

AUTOMOBILE ASSOCIATION

AA Centre 18–22 Melville St. Insurance Services 031-226 4031. Travel Agency 031-225 3301

BANKS

Allied Irish Banks 131 George St 031-226 5206. Open Mon–Fri 9.30–3.30

Bank of America 24 St Andrew Sq 031-556 5561

Bank of Credit and Commerce 3 St Andrew Sq 031-557 2720

Bank of Nova Scotia 6 South Charlotte St 031-226 3911

Bank of Scotland The Mound 031-442 7777. No charges made with National Westminster, TSB, Co-op. Open Mon–Wed & Fri 9.30–4.45, Thu 9.30–3.30 & 4.30–5.30

Barclays Bank 35 St Andrew Sq 031-557 2733. Foreign section available. Cash point inside bank open 9.15–4.45. Open Mon–Fri 9.30–3.30

British Linen Bank 4 Melville St 031-453 1919. Open Mon–Fri 9–5

Chemical Bank 17 Charlotte Sq 031-226 2987

Citibank Capital House, 2 Festival Sq 031-228 3000

Clydesdale Bank 29 George St 031-225 4081. Affiliated to the Midland Bank. Foreign section available. TSB Speedbank cards and Nat West cards must be used at cash points. Open Mon–Fri 9.30–3.30, Thu also 4.30–6

Clydesdale Bank Edinburgh Airport 031-333 3146. Bureau de change facility. Open Mon–Fri 8–7, Sat 9–4.30 (9–2.30 in winter), Sun 11–5

Co-operative Bank 15/17 South St Andrew St 031-557 3399. Open Mon–Fri 9.30–3.30

County Bank 7 Forres St 031-226 6318

Credit Lyonnais 86 George St 031-226 4324

First National Bank of Chicago 46 Charlotte Sq 031-226 5794

Hong Kong and Shanghai Banking Corporation Hobart House, 76 Hanover St 031-225 9393. Open Mon–Thu 9.30–12.30 & 1.30–3.30 (closes 4.30 Mon), Fri 9.30–3.30

Lloyds Bank 113/115 George St 031-226 4021. Foreign section available. Cash points situated outside bank. Open Mon–Fri 9.30–3.30

Lombard North Central 20 Dublin St 031-557 3434

National Girobank 93 George St 031-226 4301. Open Mon–Fri 9–5.30

National Westminster Bank 80 George St 031-226 6181. Affiliated with Midland Bank and Ulster Bank. Cash point outside bank (Midland cash cards can be used). Open Mon–Fri 9.30–3.30

Royal Bank of Scotland 42 St Andrew Sq 031-556 8555. Foreign section available. No charges made with Bank of Scotland and Nat West. Open Mon–Fri 9.30–3.30, Thu also 4.30–5.30

Société Générale 45 George St 031-225 7933

Standard Chartered Bank 18–20 George St 031-225 4615. Open Mon–Thu 9.30–12.30 & 1.30–3.30, Fri 9.30–3.30

Trustee Savings Bank of Scotland 28 Hanover St 031-226 3671. Foreign section available

BUREAUX DE CHANGE

Clydesdale Bank Bureau de Change Waverley Market

DIRECTORY 91

031-556 7306. Open May & June Mon–Sat 8.30–7.30, Sun 11–3; Jul, Aug & Sep Mon–Sat 8.30–8.30, Sun 11–3; Oct–end Apr Mon–Fri 9–5.30, Sat 9–12.30. Also at Edinburgh Airport

EMERGENCIES

In emergencies, telephone 999 and say which service is required—Fire Brigade, Police or Ambulance. There is no charge for the call. See also *Hospitals* and *Police Station*.

GUIDED TOUR SERVICES
WALKING TOURS

The Cadies Scottish Personal Guides 9 Belford Terr 031-332 3429

Countryside Ranger Service Guided Walks From the Visitor Centre, Hermitage of Braid. For programme 031-447 7145

Edinburgh Tours For details of the Royal Mile Tour 031-661 0125

Ghosts and Ghouls Two-hour evening tour from the Mercat Cross at 10pm

Guided Walks Around Historical Cramond Sunday tour Mr Gibbs 031-336 6034

Historical Edinburgh Tours Evening tours (not during Festival period) Miss J Thompson 031-346 0212

Mercat Tours Two-hour tour from the Mercat Cross, High Street, at 2.30pm

New Town Walks Details of daytime and evening walks from New Town Conservation Centre, 13a Dundas St 031-556 7054

1868 City Tours Three-hour tours of the Old Town in transport of a by-gone age. 031-334 8211

CITY COACH TOURS

For details of coach tours of the city contact:

Eastern Scottish St Andrew Square Bus Station 031-558 1616/7

Lothian Region Transport Waverley Bridge 031-226 5087

Scotline Tours 87 High St 031-557 0162

CHAUFFEUR-DRIVEN GUIDED TOURS

Ghillie Personal Travel 64 Silverknowes Rd East 031-336 3120

Scottish Tours 66 Cumberland St 031-556 0352

W L Sleigh Ltd 99 Shandwick Pl 031-226 3080

HEALTH
CHEMIST

Boots the Chemist 48 Shandwick Pl 031-225 6757. Open Mon–Sat 8am–9pm, Sun 11am–4.30pm

EMERGENCY DENTAL SERVICE

Accident and Emergency Department Western General Hospital, Crewe Rd South 031-332 2525. Emergency service is available 7.30pm–10.30pm daily. At other times contact the **Edinburgh Dental Hospital** 31 Chambers St 031-225 9511 or the General Dental Practitioner Services

HOSPITALS

24-hour accident and emergency

Royal Infirmary of Edinburgh 1 Lauriston Place 031-229 2477

Western General Hospital Crewe Rd South 031-332 2525

For non-emergency medical treatment contact the nearest General Practitioner. Most hotels and guesthouses will have a list of addresses.

LIBRARIES

Central Library George IV Bridge 031-225 5584

Fountainbridge Library 137 Dundee St 031-229 4588

McDonald Road Library corner of McDonald Rd and Leith Walk 031-556 5630

Morningside Library 184 Morningside Rd 031-447 1180

National Library of Scotland George IV Bridge 031-226 4531

Stockbridge Library Hamilton Pl 031-332 2173

NEWSAGENTS

International Newsagents 367 High St 031-225 4827

John Menzies
107 Princes St, G2
10b Queensferry St, G2
31 Holm St, Tolcross
197 Whitehouse Rd, G4
6 Bridge Rd, G13
26 Elm Row, G7
65 St James Centre, G1

NEWSPAPERS

Morning daily
Daily Record
Glasgow Herald
Scottish Daily Express
The Scotsman

Evening daily
Evening News

Weekly
Scottish Sunday Express
Sunday Mail
Sunday Post

PHOTOGRAPHY

Magic Moments 151 Gilmore Pl 031-229 7217. Same-day developing

Photo Lab Express 103 Princes St 031-225 1468. 24-hr developing

POLICE STATION

Lothian & Borders Police Headquarters Fettes Ave 031-311 3131. (Includes lost property)

POST OFFICES

Edinburgh Head Post Office 2–4 Waterloo Pl, Edinburgh EH1 1AA 031-550 8200

Boroughmuirhead P O 1 Merchiston Pl, Edinburgh EH10 4NP 031-229 2857

Forrest Road P O 33 Forrest Rd, Edinburgh EH1 2QP 031-225 3957

Frederick Street P O, 40 Frederick St, Edinburgh EH2 1EY 031-226 6937

Hope Street P O 7 Hope St, Edinburgh EH2 4EN 031-225 7433

Leith Walk P O 263a Leith Walk, Edinburgh EH6 8NY 031-554 2988

Newington P O 41 South Clerk St, Edinburgh EH8 9NZ 031-667 1154

Tollcross P O 5 Brougham St, Edinburgh EH3 9JS 031-229 8536

Tyncastle P O 66 Gorgie Rd, Edinburgh EH11 2NB 031-337 3673

TV AND RADIO

TELEVISION STATIONS

BBC Television
Scottish Television
Channel Four

RADIO

BBC Radio Services Radio Scotland 370m 810kHz 92.5–94.6 MHz

IBA Radio Services Radio Forth 194m 1548kHz 97.3 MHz

TOILETS

The following toilets, situated in the city centre, are open 9am–6pm and have facilities for the disabled.

Canongate (foot of the Royal Mile)

Castle Terrace Car Park

Haymarket

The Mound Princes St

Ross Open-Air Theatre Princes St Gardens (open May–Sep)

Waverley Market Princes St (open 24hrs)

TOURIST INFORMATION CENTRES

Edinburgh Festival Fringe 170 High St, EH1 1QS 031-226 5257

Edinburgh Festival Society 21 Market St, EH1 1BW 031-226 4001

Edinburgh Internationl Jazz Festival 116 Canongate, EH8 8DD 031-557 1642

Edinburgh Military Tattoo, The Tattoo Office, 22 Market St, EH1 1QB 031-225 1188

The National Trust for Scotland 5 Charlotte Sq, EH2 4DU 031-226 5922

Scottish Arts Council Arts Information Centre 19 Charlotte Sq, EH2 4DF 031-226 6051. Open Mon–Thu 9–5.30, Fri. 9–5. Information on concerts, exhibitions, festivals, dance and drama etc. in Edinburgh and elsewhere in Scotland

Scottish Development Department Historic Buildings and Monuments Division, 20 Brandon St 031-556 8400

Scottish Tourist Board 23 Ravelston Terr, EH4 3TP 031-332 2433. No personal callers, telephone enquiries only

Scottish Travel Centre South St Andrews St 031-332 2433. Personal callers welcome

Tourist Information and Accommodation Centre Waverley Market, Princes St, EH2 2QP 031-557 2727

Tourist Information Centre Edinburgh Airport 031-333 2167

ANNUAL EVENTS

February	**International Rugby** at Murrayfield
March	**International Rugby** at Murrayfield
April	**Edinburgh Folk Festival**
June	**Royal Highland and Agricultural Show** at Ingliston
August	**Edinburgh Book Festival**
	Edinburgh Festival Fringe
	Edinburgh Film Festival
	Edinburgh International Festival
	Edinburgh Jazz Festival
	Edinburgh Military Tattoo

Pocket Guide AA INDEX

Main entries are shown in **bold**
Entries for places outside the city of Edinburgh generally refer
to 'places of interest' listed in the Directory section

A

accommodation 79
Adam, Robert 18, 21, 67
Adam, William 20, 67
air services 79
annual events 92
antique shops 88
around Edinburgh 83
Arthur's seat **54**
Automobile Association 90

B

Balfour, Andrew 40
banks 90
Baxter's Tolbooth 70
Bell, Alexander Graham 74
Bonnie Prince Charlie 16, 17, 32, 51
Book Festival 36
bookshops 88
bowling greens 86
Bridges in Edinburgh **46**, **64–5**, 71
British Rail 79, 90
Brodie, Deacon William 24, 43, 75
bureaux de change 90
Burns, Robert 18, 23, 25, 42
bus services 89
by road 79

C

Calton Cemetery 21, 65
Calton Hill 21, **48**, 64–65
Camera Obscura 24, **46**
camping and caravanning 80
Cannon Ball House 23
Canongate, The 19, 22, 28
Canongate Church 28, **46**
Canongate Tolbooth 28, **46**
car hire 89
car parks 90
casinos 85
Chambers, William 21
Charles I 13, 23
Charles II 16
Charlotte Square 20, 21, 42, **47**
churches in Edinburgh 47
cinemas 85
City Art Centre 37, 47
City Chambers 20, 49
coach services 79
Cockburn Association 22
Cockburn, Lord Henry 41
Colinton 29, 49
Commonwealth Games 18
Conan Doyle, Sir Arthur 43
Corstorphine 49
Corstorphine Church 20
craft shops 88
Craig, James 20, 66
Craigmillar Castle 49
Cramond **29**, **50**, **68–9**

D

Dean Village **30**, **50**, **70**
Defoe, Daniel 16, 27
delicatessens 89
discos 85
dry cleaner 89
Duddingston 32, **50**
Dundas, Henry 41

E

eating and drinking out 81
Edinburgh Castle 16, 22, **50**
Edinburgh Central Library 64
Edinburgh International Festival 18, 34
Edinburgh Zoo 52

94 INDEX

emergencies 91
entertainment 85
Erskine, Thomas 41

―――――― F ――――――

Fergusson, Robert 17, 23, 26, 28, 42
Film Festival 36, 37
fishing 86
Flodden 14
football 86
Forbes, Duncan 41
Fringe, The 36
Fruitmarket Gallery 37, 47

―――――― G ――――――

George IV Bridge 24, 64
George Heriot's School 14, **52**, 67
Georgian House, The 47, **52**
Gladstone's Land 19, 24, **52**
golf courses 86
Grassmarket, The 22, **52**, 53
Gregory, Professor James 28, 43
Greyfriars Bobby 53, **66**–**7**
Greyfriars Church **53**, 66
Greyfriars Churchyard 19, 66
greyhound racing 87
guesthouses 80
guided tours services 91

―――――― H ――――――

Haig, Douglas, Earl 74
health 91
Heart of Midlothian 53
Henry VIII 13, 15
Heriot, George 39, 52
Heriot's Hospital 20, 21
Hillend Ski Centre 53
Holyrood Abbey 13, 28
Holyrood, Castle of 13
Holyroodhouse, Palace of 13, 28
Holyrood Park 54
horse racing 87
hotels 79
Hume, David 21, 23, 24, 42
Huntly House 19, 28, **54**

―――――― I, J ――――――

ice sports 87
James III 13
James IV 13
James VI (I of England) 15
James VII (II of England) 13, 16, 40
Jazz Festival 36, 37
John Knox House 19, 27, **55**

―――――― K, L ――――――

Knox, John 25, **38**
Lady Stair's House 24, **55**
Lauriston Castle 40, **55**
Lawnmarket, The 53
Leith **31**, **55**
libraries 91
light meals and snacks 81
Lind, James 43
Lister, James 18, 43
Livingstone, David 72
Lorimer, Sir Robert 22

―――――― M ――――――

Macdonald, Flora 16, 26
Mackintosh, Charles Rennie 22
Malleny Gardens 55
Martyrs' Monument 66
Mary, Queen of Scots 15, 25, **38**, 49, 58
Meadowbank Sports Centre **56**
Meadows, The **56**
Mercat Cross 26
motor racing 87
Mound, The **56**
Museum of Childhood 22, 27, **56**

―――――― N ――――――

Napier, John 38
Nasmyth, Alexander 17, 42
National Gallery of Scotland 37, **56**, 73
National Library of Scotland **56**, 64
National Museums of Scotland **57**
National Trust for Scotland 24, 47
Newhaven 32
newsagents 91
newspapers 91
New Town **74**–**5**
night clubs 85
Nor' Lock 18, 65
North Bridge 65

―――――― O ――――――

Old College, The 65
Old Town, The 17, 19, 20, 23
other recommended hotels 80
other recommended restaurants 81
Outlook Tower 24

―――――― P ――――――

Palace of Holyrood, The 20, 38, **57**
Parliament Hall 20
Parliament House 25, **58**
photography 91
pitch and putt 87
places to visit 44–62, 81
Playfair, William H 21, 56
police station 91

pony trekking 87
Portobello **59**
post offices 91
Princes Street and Gardens **59**, **72–3**
pub food 81
pubs with entertainment 85
putting 87

―――――― Q, R ――――――

Queensberry House 28
Raeburn, Sir Henry 17, 42
Ramsay, Allan 17, 23, 27, 42
recreation 86
Regent Bridge 65
Register House 21, 42, **59**, 72
Reid, General John 41
restaurants 81
Riddle's Court 19
riding 87
rivers 86
Roman Fort 69
Royal Bank of Scotland 76
Royal Botanic Gardens 40, **59**
Royal Commonwealth Pool **60**
Royal High School **60**
Royal Mile 12, 13, 23
Royal Museum of Scotland 64
Royal Observatory **60**
Royal Scottish Academy 37, 73
rugby 87

―――――― S ――――――

St Andrew's and St George's Church **47**, 76
St Cuthbert's Church **47**
St Giles 20, 25, 27, 38, **60**
St John's Church 24, 73
St Margaret's Chapel 19
St Mary's Cathedral **47**
St Stephen's Church **47**
Scott, Sir Walter 18, 25, 42, 67, 75
Scott Monument **60**, 72
Scottish Agricultural Museum **61**
Scottish Craft Centre 28
Scottish evenings 85
Scottish National Gallery of Modern Art 37, 61

Scottish Poetry Library 28
sea and shore 86
self-catering 80
shopping 88
Simpson, Sir James Young 43, 73, 75
skiing 87
Smith, Adam 23
snooker 87
sports 86
sports centres 88
Stevenson, Robert Louis 25, 42, 61, 75
Stockbridge **31**
Swanston **33**, **61**
swimming 88

―――――― T ――――――

tartans and woollens 89
taxis 90
Telford, Thomas 42, 50
theatres and concert halls 85
toilets 92
tourist information centres 92
trains 79
transport 89
Tron Church **61**
TV and radio 92

―――――― U ――――――

useful information 90
University of Edinburgh 41, **61**
Usher Hall **62**

―――――― W ――――――

Water of Leith 49, **62**, **70–1**
Waverley Market 72
Wax Museum 26, 41, **62**
West Register House **62**, 74
White Horse Close 28, **62**

―――――― Y ――――――

Youth Hostels 80
YMCA 80
YWCA 80

Opening doors to the World of books

BOOK TOKEN

Book Tokens

Book Tokens can be bought and exchanged at most bookshops